Jubilee

on Wall Street

Jubilee
on
Wall
Street

An Optimistic Look at the Coming Financial Crash

by
David Knox Barker

Prescott Press
Lafayette, Louisiana

4 5 6 7 8 9 10

Prescott Press, Lafayette, Louisiana
Typography and cover design by Publications Technologies
Printed in the United States of America

*Distributed by Huntington House, Inc.
P.O. Box 53788, Lafayette, LA 70505*

Contents

Contents

Dedication

In Loving Memory of Mom

Nancy Boyd Barker

Acknowledgements

A very special note of thanks must go out to Dr. Edward Allen whose love of teaching is largely responsible for my love of learning. The mark of a great educator is the admiration, respect and love of his students which Dr. Allen selflessly inspires year after year. Appreciation must be extended to Dr. Ray Jones and Dr. Mike Schellenger, who presented me with the financial and economic foundations on which to build. And to Dr. Jawad Barghothi to whom I am indebted for showing me that I can indeed learn to like a liberal. Last but not least I readily confess that without the support of my entire family, this book would have never been written; especially my brilliant sister Nan whose proof of my first draft was no doubt a trying job.

Preface

*Every fiftieth year let the trumpets blow loud and long
throughout the land. For the fiftieth year shall be holy, a time
to proclaim liberty throughout the land to all enslaved debtors,
and a time for the canceling of all public and private debts. It
shall be a year when all the family estates sold to others shall
be returned to the original owners or their heirs.*

*What a happy year it will be! In it you shall not sow, nor
gather crops nor grapes; for it is a holy Year of Jubilee for you.
That year your food shall be the volunteer crops that grow wild
in the fields. Yes, during the Year of Jubilee everyone shall return home to his original family possession; if he has sold it, it
shall be his again!*

*Because of this, if the land is sold or bought during the
preceding forty-nine years, a fair price shall be arrived at by
counting the number of years until the Jubilee. If the Jubilee is
many years away, the price will be high; if few years, the price
will be low; for what you are really doing is selling the number
of crops the owner will get from the land before it is returned
to you.*

*You must fear your God and not overcharge! For I am Je-
hovah. Obey my laws if you want to live safely in the land.
When you obey, the land will yield bumper crops and you can
eat your fill in safety.*

— Leviticus 25: 8-19
The Living Bible

Introduction

On Monday, January 20, 1986 *The Wall Street Journal* ran a front-page article which discussed the potential existence of a 50- to 60-year cycle of "boom and bust" in the world economy. This was only one of many similar articles that has surfaced in recent months in numerous newspapers and magazines. To the surprise of many the *Wall Street Journal* article mentions a number of prominent economists and institutions that take very seriously the evidence of a long-wave economic cycle.

Even as the stock markets of the world are exploding to new heights there is a growing belief that the world economy is currently on a "knife edge of instability" and that forces from any number of sectors in the economy will eventually push us over the edge and into a major depression. Among the institutions that are interested in the long-wave cycle is the prominent Massachusetts Institute of Technology which has an entire program dedicated to studying the cycle. The program at MIT is sponsored by dozens of major international corporations that, for very obvious reasons, are extremely interested in the long-wave economic cycle.

There is a fascinating dimension to the cycle that the recent *Wall Street Journal* article and others are not discussing. Over 4,000 years ago, forces were acknowledged and defined that if left unchecked in a free-market economy will eventually lead to a severe depression and financial collapse every half-century. The source of these early warnings gives the long-wave theory an unexpected yet prominent and respected endorsement.

God gave us a clear outline of the dangerous forces and elements that create the long-wave cycle when He presented the Old Testament laws for the Year of Jubilee. According to Old Testament law, The Year of Jubilee was to take place every 50 years. It was to prevent the build-up of inefficient and dangerous elements in the economy that lead to economic collapse.

13

will not attempt to define a strict relationship be-
e Year of Jubilee and our free-market economy's long-
le. The principles presented by The Year of Jubilee are
used ly as a foundation and theme for our study and observations.

The reader should know at this early point that this book was
not written to suggest a radical change to the structure of our economic system. In a real sense this book will applaud our free-
market system as being very close to the best man can hope to
achieve. This book is simply an attempt to present and underscore
the inherent elements within our system that were acknowledged
in the Old Testament and which of necessity will eventually lead
our free-market economy into depression. God had the foresight to
see that our competitiveness would eventually cause a free-market
system to get ahead of itself and out of control.

The situation is not so bad as it sounds. There is a bright
side to the gloomy picture we are painting. The fact is that the
same inherent elements that cause the collapse are what give our
free-market system its vitality and strength. The natural forces
within our free-market system always bring it back stronger
than ever shortly after its predictable decline.

One potential problem that was clearly pointed out by the
laws for the Year of Jubilee is that as human nature is combined
with a free market we have a tendency to take on too much debt.
This is why all public and private debts were forgiven and erased
in The Year of Jubilee. Every 50 years the economy was given a
new foundation on which to build. We are all aware that when
debt is used as liberally as it is in our free-market system it invariably causes rising prices. This is because the interest charged
on debt increases the costs of production. Continually rising
prices eventually coax industry into overexpansion.

This overexpansion is financed with increasingly expensive
debt. Debt begins playing an ever-increasing role in the economy.
As overexpansion spreads throughout the entire economy we
soon have far too much production capacity. This excess capacity
leads to overproduction in virtually every industry. When you
have too many products being chased by falling demand, you
will of necessity have falling prices — except for stock prices,
which begin surging during the initial period of deflation.

Falling prices in an overexpanded economy that is loaded
with expensive debt will eventually lead to only one thing —
depression. The depression cleans the inefficiencies out of the
system and brings a collapse in the stock markets. Inefficient

debt that has built up over the years is erased by default and bankruptcies. Continually collapsing prices are brought on by the ensuing depression. Our free-market economy is purged by the depression and given a new foundation on which to build — which was the exact purpose of The Year of Jubilee. After the depression our economy begins the next advance and we go through our expanding and eventually overexpanding process all over again — taking some 50 years to complete the cycle.

Just look around the economy today and you see overproduction in virtually every industry. Agriculture, energy (oil) and textiles are only three examples of the many industries that are overproducing today. This is naturally leading the world economy into an environment of falling prices — just as we saw in the 20s. One major difference between The Year of Jubilee and our modern economy's long-wave cycle is that the Jubilee system took only one year to effectively do its job whereas our system may take a decade of depression before the inefficiency is purged from the system and we are ready to start the next advance.

There is another important aspect to The Year of Jubilee that is also directly related to prices. All land was to be returned to its original owner in The Year of Jubilee. If all land is returned to its original owner in year 50 you would certainly be more willing to pay a higher price for land in year one than in year 49. Land was the chief means of production in those days. In a Jubilee system all prices in the economy would have been controlled by having the price for the land constantly falling.

We are beginning to see that in the Jubilee system the elements that cause the collapse in our economy: debt, prices and expansion would have all been controlled. You would have the highest prices and highest debt in year one of a Jubilee system and they would decrease consistently until reaching zero in the 50th year. We see the exact opposite occurring in our free-market system as we have low prices and little debt early in the cycle. When we approach the end of the cycle we have our highest prices and our largest amounts of debt. High prices and outrageous debt precipitate the collapse of our free-market system. In a system such as Jubilee, the economy would not have to correct itself through a collapse as the modern free-market system has been observed to do.

Of course the economic system during Old Testament days was far simpler than our system today. Virtually all of the economy's production was connected to the land which made a

Jubilee system viable. The world economy is far more complex today, but the basic principles and problems God revealed through The Year of Jubilee still apply — we are still human.

The first person to discover and study this long-wave cycle in relation to our modern free-market economy was, ironically, a Russian economist by the name of Nikolai Kondratieff. Kondratieff was working on the first five year agricultural plan under Stalin and was studying Western grain production and prices when he first stumbled onto the long-wave cycle. After taking a close look at the data he had collected, he began to see the emergence of the long-wave cycle in all prices and production. He was fascinated with this phenomenon and began to study other variables such as interest rates and labor and saw that they also followed the long-wave pattern. Kondratieff did extensive research on the cycle and published his findings in 1926. Kondratieff was convinced of a long-wave cycle of boom and bust in the capitalist system. Stalin was, of course, very pleased with the notion of the inevitable collapse of the Western world's economic system. He was infuriated with Kondratieff's findings that the system would rebound from its collapse and come back even stronger than ever in it's next advance — after being purged of its inefficiencies.

Kondratieff's research showed distinct long-wave cycles from 1789 until his research in the early 1920s. Kondratieff was rewarded for his research by his imprisonment in a slave-labor camp where he died in 1938. His death came only after his predicted economic collapse of the West had begun in the form of the Great Depression. Alexander Solzhenitsyn recorded the death of Kondratieff in his book *The Gulag Archipelago*.

As we begin our study it should be remembered that the late 1920s saw the financial markets of the world reaching all-time highs and the investing public in a state of euphoria. Great profits were being realized by investors as the stock market reached levels never before dreamed possible. Very few had the insight to see what was just ahead and not even those few realized the depth to which the world economy would soon sink. Nikolai Kondratieff was one man who had seen and predicted what was to come — but the world would not listen. Once again the economic prophecies of the forgotten Russian are coming to fruition and once again the world is not listening.

We are all aware of the market crash of 1929 and the depression of the 1930s. Around the year 1939, as we entered the second world war, the world was once again working its way out of a decline of the long-wave cycle. Since then we have been in an advancing economy that has seen rising prices and debt. The early 1980s saw a peak in real prices of commodities and raw materials. This has always marked the principal peak in economic expansion of the long-wave cycle. The peak in expansion has always preceded the peak in the financial world and money markets by a decade. Just as in the 1920s we are currently on the plateau period of the long wave.

This plateau has pushed us into one last fling in the financial markets before we are pushed over the edge. This last fling began with the bull market in 1982. The next few years will offer opportunities in the financial markets that are available only once in a lifetime. It is important that we not look to confine the long wave to a strict 50 years but acknowledge that it must have room to fluctuate due to being such a large cycle.

Kondratieff said the long wave fluctuates between 45 and 60 years with an average of approximately 50 — thus we must not be rigid in our interpretations and projections. Keeping this in mind we can begin to look ahead in an attempt to interpret what the future may hold.

Although the late 70s and early 80s marked the peak in long wave expansion, the late 80s will see the peak in the stock markets of the world along with many other shifts and changes in the financial world.

One such change may well be the collapse of the international monetary system and the introduction of a new system. The long wave cannot be predicted with pinpoint accuracy in the financial markets and the collapse could come at any time. Once the financial collapse occurs, the collapse of the economy will soon follow.

When studying an all-encompassing subject like the long-wave cycle we must remember that the world economy is much like a great work of art. Standing too close while viewing a masterpiece, one gets a distorted view of the message the master intended. A narrow, shortsighted view tends to emphasize one aspect while diminishing the value of the whole. We are all products of a system that, while at times attempting to deliver a holistic experience, fails miserably. We all find our comfortable niche in which we feel at ease and would seem to have satisfied all our needs and desires.

At the same time we are given a sense of contribution to the whole of society. Whether a lawyer, accountant, minister, chemist, doctor, banker, broker, teacher, historian, physicist, poet or sage we are all guilty of underexposure to the whole of life. This distorts our perception of the world economy and the vital role played by the sum total of its diverse elements.

After a long hike through rugged terrain I once found myself standing on the edge of a large river observing a fisherman who had waded into the center and was proceeding to cast his line. In curiosity of my location I called out to him and asked which direction at that point the river was flowing, be it north, south, east, or west. The man's reply was simple and told a story all too telling of our condition today. He said, "Sir," with a smile on his face, "I couldn't tell as it is really of no concern to me, I am here simply to catch my limit for the day and return home."

We are all guilty of making our daily catch with no concern for the directional flow of the economic river that is providing for our existence. Within the confines of our well-known and understood fishing hole we are not able to ascertain that a few hours earlier there was flash flooding in the plains upriver and at this moment there are high waters making their way down to our quite undisturbed fishing hole. We are equally unaware that just downstream there is the precipitous drop of a 500-foot waterfall and being caught unprepared we will be carried on the rising water to our ultimate ruin and downfall.

The purpose of this book is not that I seek reputation as a prophet of doom or a fortuneteller. I am a historical realist who also happens to be an incurable optimist. This book is an effort to show the reader that, being fully aware and prepared for the long-wave economic cycle, he should use it to his advantage.

This book will ask you to step back from the masterpiece and take in the entire meaning the master was attempting to relate. I will ask you to look beyond your fishing hole to question what the snows were like in the mountains in late spring and what the summer rains will bring. Our masterpiece and river, the world economy, consist of complexities and intricacies from the price of gold to the explosion of technology, from open trade to trade wars, from nations living beyond their means to nations struggling without any means. I will attempt to interweave all elements of 200 years of indisputable history.

This book takes a very fundamental approach to the long-wave cycle. I have avoided burdening the reader with technical analysis and statistical data.

Cycle theory is fascinating and intriguing and makes enjoyable reading; it is my hope this book is no exception. This book was written to make you consider your current position and where you would like to find yourself in the coming years. There is no reason to fear the long-wave cycle; if used correctly, obstacles only enhance and advance one's position. A true winner is sharpened by adversity and is made all the stronger through trials. I am convinced of the long-wave cycle and will seek to relate to you how best to weather the winter and strengthen your position while the world economy enters its predictable decline. The picture this book will paint is not a pretty one — but a real one. However, as surely as winter follows fall, so the winter of necessity gives birth to spring. During the difficult days ahead we must maintain a long-term perspective and keep in mind God's view of the long-wave cycle, "A Jubilee shall that 50th year be to you."

1

A Haunting Past

Any theory that attempts to put forward the notion that history will undoubtedly and of necessity repeat itself must first acknowledge history as its primary instrument of research.

Part I:
Laying a Foundation

Clearly this is the case with the long-wave cycle as the observation of history plays an all-important role in our study. We will readily admit that our chief concern in attempting to prove the existence of the long-wave cycle lies in our most recent or modern history of the past 200 years. But to limit our observations to modern history alone would be closed minded and intellectually dangerous.

This chapter looks deep into the history of man so that we may gain a broad-based perspective and a clear and well-rounded understanding of the issues we will be dealing with. We would not want to be accused of being near-sighted historians and economists.

There are those who have traced evidence of a long-wave cycle reaching back well over a thousand years into the Dark Ages and there is some substantial evidence to support these claims. But our purpose in looking beyond the past 200 years is not for proof and evidence of the long wave. We will clearly and effectively establish proof of the long wave with our review of modern history.

Our reason for looking beyond the modern period is an effort to gain greater insight into economic decline and collapse. The declines we will review in this chapter played an all-important role in molding the world we live in today. The recorded declines of ancient history have haunting similarities with modern history's declines and depressions. There is no doubt that we can learn a great deal about ourselves and about our future by looking deep into our past.

Many have a hard time imagining the Pharaoh of Egypt in the year 2500 B.C. pacing his pyramid worried over the current trade imbalance or the dwindling of the treasury due to extravagant public works projects. Whether due to our preoccupation with the present or simply a lack of education, it would seem there is a prevailing view that ups and downs in the economy are a fairly modern problem facing mankind. The fact of the matter is that for thousands of years man has been plagued with the seeming uncontrollable economic downturn just when life was beginning to suit him.

Just what are the forces that cause kings to fall from their thrones, banks to shut their doors and sane men to leap from tall buildings? Are there natural laws that govern the rise and fall of economic elements or does man have the sole key that controls the forces that can and will bring whole nations and civilizations to their knees?

To begin our search for the answers to these questions and others let us look back over the annals of time to acquire a historical perspective of the rise and the inevitable fall of the economic cycle.

The noted historian Otto C. Lightner published a major work entitled *The History of Economic Depressions.* This work gives an insightful perspective into the problem of changing economic forces and the havoc they played on man's plans hundreds and even thousands of years ago.

This chapter is to be a brief and hopefully entertaining overview of the Ancient, Medieval and Renaissance history of man's conflict with his economy. We will look at a number of fascinating facts and stories. Most of the stories and quotes found in this chapter come from the work of Lightner who had a powerful style coupled with piercing insight. This chapter is meant to build a foundation and be somewhat of a preview before we get into our study of long-wave theory.

We will begin our quest for answers on the ancient shores of the Mediterranean Sea. Going as far back as 4000 B.C., the Mesopotamians had made great advances in civilization. They engaged in substantial trade and commerce and some historians say they had banks similar to those of the present day. Around the year 2000 B.C., the Babylonian people grew to great importance as a commercial nation. The Assyrians emerged from the carnage left from Babylonian demise. During the first millennium B.C.

disorganization and then anarchy came to the Assyrians and the Persians became the dominant and ruling people.

It would be fascinating to have a documented historical account of the demise and destruction of these ancient empires. Perhaps it was a few dry years and the devastation of the wheat harvest that brought the Assyrians to ruin; possibly the Persian leaders had an extravagance for villas on the Mediterranean and a weakness for wine and women. Even without perfect records we know that there were major shifts taking place in the commerce of the world that led to the fall and decline of these empires.

In considering the decline of Babylon we see this clearly. "It was only when the Europeans found a new path to India across the ocean and converted the great commerce of the world from a land to a sea trade that the royal city on the banks of the Tigris and Eurphrates began to decline. Then, deprived of its commerce it fell a victim to the two-fold oppression of anarchy and violence and sunk to its original state — a stinking marsh and barren land," according to Lightner.

It would be easy to drift into the dangerous game of finding one villain for all the problems and afflictions that bring about the rise and fall of civilizations. Every factor plays its role and is only enhanced and strengthened by other elements as they slowly weave their way together and around the very life of the civilization they are seeking to destroy. According to Lightner, "Following Babylon, the Phoenicians developed a great society and extensive commerce about 1500 B.C. Then the Heroic Age of Greece brought that country to commercial supremacy. Later came the great Roman Empire and domination of the world and with it the greatest and longest period of peace and prosperity the world has ever known. The Romans were great organizers and skilled administrators. Then under the Caesars with its corruption came decline in commerce and the scepter of Roman authority passed from the western world."

The rise and fall of civilizations beyond the control of their subject man was not confined to the Mediterranean region. Our counterparts of the Far East were not immune from the disease of decline that infects all men who have come together to form both political and economic ties in their quest to build a stable society. "From the scraps that we have been able to sift from the history of China it is apparent that that ancient and interesting people had periods of great trade decline and depression from causes that we are unable now to discover," wrote Lightner. "Otherwise how could she allow such inventions as the printing press and the mariners compass to be forgotten and obliterated, once they had been discovered and used."

In most cases in ancient times the God of the rise and fall granted but one soul to a civilization to be filled to overflowing only to be brought down and destroyed forever. The first known exception to the one soul rule was that of ancient Egypt. Egypt is the first clear example of a society whose economy repeatedly rose and fell yet maintained its identity as a nation. "In its day ancient Egypt at times basked in the sunshine of luxury and in periods of depression she put armies of unemployed to work and fed them while they built the pyramids. We know that the history of ancient Egypt was marked by four declines and revivals and at no time during this period was she conquered, so in those periods, when the records are almost entirely obliterated there must have been widespread economic distress," according to Lightner.

The Greeks are known for their innovation in politics and philosophy and for their openness and creative spirit in dealing with the issues and obstacles facing man. For thousands of years man had attempted to avert the erosion of faith in his existing commercial system unsuccessfully; but in the year 594 B.C. Solon of Athens took radical measures never before recorded. The plan Solon used to bring order to Greece's economy is very much like the plan laid out for The Year of Jubilee. Whether Solon borrowed the plan or came upon it spontaneously, its application as a cure for a worsening situation was unique. While The Year of Jubilee was to be applied as preventive medicine, Solon was applying his plan as Athens lay on her death bed.

"The great depression of 594 B.C. when Solon came forward in a time of public distress and rescued the Athenians from a most serious situation, marks an epoch in the economic history of ancient times," noted Lightner. "Debt and poverty oppressed the poor citizens and melancholy, indeed is the picture which historians draw of the social state of Athens at that time. Among the higher classes there prevailed a spirit of selfish greed whose greatest aim seemed to be to oppress the poor and wring from them their last farthing (dime). So terrible was the depression that Solon perceived great dangers. People were ready to do anything to better their condition and powerful neighbors were getting ready to take advantage of the situation to attack Athens. Solon by birth belonged to the aristocracy, but his fortunes had thrown him among merchants and there he gained knowledge of the causes, as well as the needed remedies for the

distress. Solon averted the impending crisis. 'His first measure
was the famous *Seisachtheia*. Every citizen who had been sold
into slavery, at home or abroad, was restored to liberty, all
debts secured upon the person or landed property of the debtors
were cancelled and for the future no one was allowed to lend
money on the security of the debtor's person.'

"All lands burdened with debt were relieved of the incum-
brance. It is a mark in history that the law enacted at that time
by Solon has been re-enacted almost exactly by different nations
on up to modern times in periods of economic depression," according to Lightner.

It was many years after Solon had saved Athens from her
distress with his radical changes and innovations that Greek civilization finally succumbed and fell from dominance in the ancient world. It was during this period that Rome began to
emerge as the dominant political and economic force in the
world as the Holy Roman Empire conquered and expanded its
borders to engulf the entire civilized world. The Roman Empire
has yet to be challenged as the greatest power in the history of
man as it dominated the world for close to 1,000 years. The stability that comes from centralization and economic interrelationship should be noted as we look at the Roman Empire. From
500 B.C. to the year 476 A.D., when she was finally sacked by
the Germanic Barbarians, Rome was the seat of government and
the *Via Sacra* was the Wall Street of the world.

Many attribute the fall of Rome to over taxation which
disgruntled the people and caused unrest allowing the Barbarians
easy victories as they moved toward Rome. The overtaxation and
growing inefficiencies of the great bureaucracy had dramatic effects on trade as the volume of the Empire's trade began to
slow. We are beginning to see the powerful force of economics
as it is the chief element in the making of man's history.

There is a popular belief that moral decadence and the erosion of a nation's value system is the cause of decline. The decline of Rome is often attributed to this erosion of values. There
is definitely evidence that supports this hypothesis. Too much
success can remove the competitive edge from a society and lead
to a lazy, pleasure-seeking mentality.

There is no doubt that an erosion of values destroys the internal structure of an economic system which will eventually
lead to the fall of the civilization. This was certainly evident in
the fall of The Roman Empire. We must be cautious as we look
for the cause of decline and not narrow our vision to any one

element. All factors must be taken into consideration as we study the forces that move the world economy.

Before moving on with our brief review of economic history into the Middle Ages, let's take a closer look at Rome. We are beginning to see that we can gain very enlightening insight into today's problems by taking a close look at similar situations in history. We can gain a number of such insights from an account of a Roman crisis in the year 33 A.D. as told by Lightner.

"When we make a hasty survey of the Roman Empire to find the symptoms of decay there is brought to light as the outstanding feature industrial stagnation and commercial ruin. The year 33 A.D. was full of events in the ancient world. It marked two disturbances as the outgrowth of the mob spirit. The first was in the remote province of Judea, where one Christus was tried before Pontius Pilate, was crucified, dead and buried. The other event was the great Roman panic which shook the empire from end to end. The consternation accompanying the latter died down and it was soon forgotten, but the murmurings of the former swept down the centuries until, bursting into flames, it enveloped the world.

"A description of the panic reads like one of our own times: The important firm of Seuthes and Son, of Alexandria, was facing difficulties because of the loss of three richly laden ships in a Red Sea storm, followed by a fall in the value of ostrich feathers and ivory. About the same time the great house of Malchus and Co. of Tyre with branches at Antioch and Ephesus, suddenly became bankrupt as a result of a strike among their Phoenician workmen and the embezzlements of a freedman manager. These failures affected the Roman banking house, *Quintus Maximus* and *Lucius Vibo.* A run commenced on their bank and spread to other banking houses that were said to be involved, particularly the Brothers Pittius. The *Via Sacra* was the Wall Street of Rome and this thoroughfare was teeming with excited merchants. These two firms looked to other bankers for aid, as is done today. Unfortunately, rebellion had occurred among the semi-civilized people of North Gaul, where a great deal of Roman capital had been invested, and a moratorium had been declared by the government on account of the disturbed conditions. Other bankers, fearing the suspended conditions, refused to aid the first two houses and this augmented the crisis.

"Money was tight for another reason: agriculture had been on a decline for some years and Tiberius had proclaimed that one-third of every senator's fortune must be invested in lands within the province of Italy in order to recoup their agricultural production.

"Publius Spintler, a wealthy nobleman, was at that time obliged to raise money to comply with the order and had called upon his bank, *Balbus Ollius,* for 30 million sesterces, which he had deposited with them. This firm immediately closed their doors and entered bankruptcy before the praetor. The panic was fast spreading throughout all the province of Rome and the civilized world. News came of the failure of the great Corinthian bank, Leucippus Sons, followed within a few days by a strong banking house in Carthage. By this time all the surviving banks on the *Via Sacra* had suspended payment to the depositors. Two banks in Lyons next were obliged to suspend; likewise, another in Byzantium. From all provincial towns creditors ran to bankers and debtors with cries of keen distress only to meet with an answer of failure or bankruptcy.

"The legal rate of interest in Rome was then 12 per cent and this rose beyond bounds. The praetor's court was filled with creditors demanding the auctioning of the debtor's property and slaves; valuable villas were sold for trifles and many men who were reputed to be rich and of large fortune were reduced to pauperism. This condition existed not only in Rome, but throughout the empire.

"Gracchus, the praetor, who saw the calamity threatening the very foundation of all the commerce and industry of the empire, dispatched a message to the emperor, Tiberius, in his villa at Capri. The merchants waited breathlessly for four days until the courier returned. The Senate assembled quickly while a vast throng, slaves and millionaires, elbow to elbow, waited in the forum outside for tidings of the emperor's action. The letter was read to the Senate then to the forum as a breath of relief swept over the waiting multitude.

"Tiberius was a wise ruler and solved the problem with his usual good sense. He suspended temporarily the processes of debt and distributed 100 million sesterces from the imperial treasury to the solvent bankers to be loaned to needy debtors without interest for three years. Following this action, the panic in Alexandria, Carthage and Corinth quieted.

"And so, under conditions very similar to those existing in the Twentieth Century, business of the Roman Empire resumed its normal aspect and the *Via Sacra* went its normal way, the same as Wall Street has done on many an occasion after the storm has passed. How similar was the business of the world in that year of the crucifixion of Christ to that of present time!"

As history rolls through the ages we see that modern man is not the only one afflicted with the changing tide of trade. Rome is a prime example. She was finally sacked by the Barbarians in 476 A.D. As the world moved from the glory days of the Roman Empire into the period known as the Middle Ages or the Dark Ages, it is hard to track the rise and fall of commerce. The years of Greek and then Roman dominance of the world were marked by great advances in art, science, literature and commerce. But starting around the year 500 A.D. the world took a radical turn for the worse which lasted for a thousand years. The ruthless reign and rampaging of the Barbarians stifled any hint of a resurrection in business or the advance of civilization. There were virtually no books written during this period and the scant trading that did exist between tribes of Western Europe was, more than not, interrupted by wars and infighting among the various peoples. The study of this period goes far to show the depth to which man can sink. "Not to be killed," says Stendhal, "and to have a good sheepskin coat in winter, was, for many people in the tenth century, the height of luxury."

During the stagnant years of the Middle Ages a new component to the economic equation was introduced. Religion, taking control of the politics of the day, soon began to have an enormous impact on commerce. The Catholic Church was becoming more and more powerful during this time and was often blamed and is still attributed for holding the world in economic bondage during this period. Wealth that was generated during this time seemed to find its way into the treasury of the Church and was spent on the extravagance of the Pope and his pious few.

However, late in the Middle Ages the tables began to turn on religion's effect on economics and an extraordinary era in the economic progress of the world was ushered in.

The Crusades were military campaigns from 1096 to 1291 that were financed by the Church and government to free the Holy Land from Islam for the Christian cause. The Crusaders did more to stimulate world trade than has any event in history before or after.

"There can be little doubt but that some were sincerely animated by a desire to wrest the Holy Land from the infidels," wrote Lightner, "but undoubtedly the great army of crusaders were homeless itinerants who had nothing to lose and all to gain. These idlers were quickly willing to fight for immediate bread and the promise of future reward. But the movement of these great armies from west to east and back again revived the industries of the nations through which they passed, created new and broadened ideas of the world's affairs, put money into circulation and started a new system of trade and commerce."

The world was slowly working its way out of its dark ages of stagnation and decline and slowly but surely a new day was dawning. The many regions and countries of the world were once again beginning to associate and trade with one another while at the same time domestic business activity was on the rise. Art and literature were beginning to emerge and there was a new view forming in support of education.

Late in the Middle Ages Holland and Spain emerged as the leading commercial countries of the Western world. There was a unique thing that was beginning to happen in these countries. The guild, which is the predecessor of today's union, came into being at this time. As early as the 15th century, depression has been attributed to the monopolistic, price fixing and protectionist policy of these guilds. The association of commercial interest as a unified front that had its beginning at this time is one of the many elements that play a role in today's rise and fall of the economic cycle. Modern debit and credit banking can be traced to the last few centuries of the Middle Ages.

"About this time the doctrine that it was sinful to take interest lost its force because economic leaders convinced the clergy that money secured through loans could be put to good use and thus encouraged legitimate development," according to Lightner.

Antwerp was recognized during this period as the financial center of the world. However, she had made the grave mistake of lending money to royal debtors who had proceeded to lose their wars and were thus incapable of repaying their loans. As history has shown, this led to a panic and depression during which the center of the financial world moved to London. And in London it remained for five centuries until the first world war when it moved to New York.

As the Middle Ages gave birth to the Renaissance, enormous changes were taking place in every area of life. Renaissance means "rebirth" and indeed this period was just that, as sweeping changes came to politics, religion and commerce. Man was beginning to find his freedom during this period as the idea of democracy surfaced for the first time since the Greeks.

It was during this time that, "we approach the age that witnessed the growing importance of the industrial and commercial classes. In former centuries laborers, no matter of what breeding or state of intelligence, were slaves. Whatever circumstances, whether the fortunes of war or the tides of trade, brought them to the state of labor they automatically became slaves," according to Lightner.

"The close of the Medieval period found man struggling upward to a state of freedom. Trade and commerce, which had been considered degrading and had been engaged in by the lower elements of mankind, was now becoming dignified and of growing importance. The old days when might was right were giving way to the time when peaceful service to humanity met its just rewards. The world emerged from feudalism because of the demands of commerce for a stronger central government to attempt to ward off the evil effects of trade declines and local depressions."

As we enter into the 16th century and the rise of the Renaissance and mercantile era, declines and depressions began to take on new characteristics. Previous to this time depressions were on the order of trade declines which moved slowly and gradually into a state of economic despair and confusion. Political folly was often the cause of these declines as is still true today, but not to the same degree as previous centuries.

As man began to find his freedom he also found his willingness to take a chance and speculate with the lot he had acquired. The art of speculation that arose during this time has stayed with us to the present and is another of the strands that weaves its way into the rope that time has shown will eventually choke the life out of the system. One of the first and certainly one of the most fascinating escapades in speculation history was centered around the years 1630 to 1635 in Holland.

"The tulip was a rare flower which had been introduced into western Europe from Turkey and grown in the horticultural collection of Counselor Herwart of Augsburg. The plants were seen by the collectors' neighbors who desired some of their own. The blooms became their pride and others were infected with the desire to possess them. Before long the single little flower had turned everything topsy-turvy; the public had caught the fever and started speculating in tulips. All Europe became involved and the flower gradually found its way at first into the gardens of wealthy people and later to all classes. Holland was the center of the tulip trade and in that country, as well as most others, it became the requisite of society to possess a collection of tulips.

"But the speculative side was probably the most romantic. The state of the people's mind was such that they wanted excitement and speculation. We read of a trader of Harlem who gave half his fortune for a single bulb. Stock jobbers made the most of the mania. Few kept their heads and fewer kept aloof from the mania. At first — and it was at this immediate period that the disease reached its virulent form — everyone had infinite confidence in the values and the speculators gained. The market broadened and, as is so often prayed for nowadays by Capel Court and Wall Street, the public came in. Everyone seemed to be making profits from tulips and no one dreamed that prices could fall. People of all grades converted their property into cash and invested in the flowers. House and lands were offered for sale at ruinous rates or assigned in payment of purchases made at the tulip market. Foreigners became smitten with the frenzy and money from abroad poured into Holland. The fever of speculation was superseded by an equally intense fever of pessimism. The whole country was involved and it became imperative that something be done to prevent general bankruptcy. The Government was appealed to. The Government did the usual thing. They discussed the matter for three months and concluded they could not solve the problems. Those who had tulips must lose and lose they did. This applied to nearly everyone. Holland suffered fearfully. Her people, many of them at least, had to begin the accumulation of savings or of fortunes all over again and for years the commerce of the nation languished."

There were numerous economic upheavals throughout Europe during the remainder of the 17th century. In 1640 Charles I sent British commerce into a tailspin by seizing the bullion deposited by the merchants in the Tower of London. In 1661 France was in great distress due to enormous trade imbalance with England, Holland and Spain. In 1672 Charles II sent shock waves through the business community by refusing payment out of the exchequer. The first modern day "run" on banks, "came when the Dutch fleet entered the Thames. When their guns were heard, consternation reigned in London. Everyone who had any money had deposited it with the goldsmiths, the bankers of those times. This money was known to have been lent to the government, which at the moment seemed to offer no security," writes Lightner.

Moving into the 18th century we had the crisis of 1720

which was the first general crisis throughout all of Europe. This crisis was precipitated by the collapse of two speculative companies supposedly organized for development in the New World. Fortunes from all over Europe were lost as the companies proved to be ivory towered. December 6th, 1745 is known as "Black Friday," according to Lightner.

"A panic spread through England based on a rumor of French invasion. A run started to withdraw *specie* (coin) from the Bank of England. The confusion was so great that all the business houses closed. But the merchants met and agreed to accept bank notes, passing a resolution urging all citizens and merchants to adopt the notes. This declaration was signed in the course of a single day by 1,140 merchants and fundholders."

England was the victim of another crisis in 1772 which brought with it 525 corporate failures. After the signing of the treaty with America, England found herself again in crisis in 1783. Cornwallis had surrendered to Washington and the British fleet had been conquered by the admiral of France. Peace brought new markets and a strain on British gold reserves and finances. The year 1789 brought with it the French Revolution and the commercial demise that was inevitable for that nation.

Coming to the close of the 18th century and looking back, we see that crises and depressions tended to be local or national in their scope of influence. On occasion we saw these downturns crossing national borders but this was the exception and not the rule. As we have discussed briefly already there are a few who claim to trace a 50-year cycle in the world's economic expansion and contraction reaching back over a thousand years.

This was done with beef and agriculture prices and although there is evidence to support this the conclusions are questionable as there is very little data available. Perhaps if detailed data was available we could see a cycle but without large amounts of sufficient information, that would be necessary to track such a cycle, it is a futile exercise. Yes, there was always a rise and fall in the world's Ancient, Middle Age and Renaissance economies, but whether an observable cycle, we will never know. Moving on into modern history where the records have been kept, this is not the case.

Beginning late in the 18th and early in the 19th century, sufficient data is available to track the emergence of a distinct, long-wave cycle in the rise and fall of the world's commerce. Many question the possibility of such a phenomenon but the evidence for its existence is overpowering. The remainder of this book will take a hard close look at the evidence for such a long-wave cycle and look into the effect such a cycle has on the investor.

First we will take a close look at modern times to which long-wave economic theory is applied and during which time we have witnessed the rise of a global world economy. We will look at the social and psychological causes and effects of the long-wave cycle and how it is related to man's armed conflict. A close look will be taken at the current world trade situation and the clues it gives us to the long-wave cycle.

Agriculture is a concern to every nation of the world and we will see how it is greatly affected by the long-wave cycle in the economy. The long wave has a great impact on the invention and implementation of new technology which we will evaluate.

Politics and how they are affected by the long wave will make for interesting discussion before we get into the heart of the matter, which is how to profit and protect our gains from our knowledge of the long wave.

We will look long and hard at the basic investment instruments of gold, stocks, bonds and real estate and how the long wave will radically affect their performance in the coming years.

Lastly, we will look at the nature of the long wave and why it is such an important and integral part of our free-market system.

2

Modern Times

For our purposes we will consider that modern times began around the time of the victory of America in her revolutionary war with England. It was approximately eight years after the Revolution that we see the beginning advance of the first long wave in cycle theory.

Before jumping into long-wave theory it would be extremely beneficial to take an overview of the period during which the cycle has emerged. In this chapter we will concentrate on the economic history of the past 200 years. This review will concentrate heavily, though not entirely, on the United States due to the availability of data and the undeniable position of the United States as leader in the world economy.

Following on the heels of the Revolutionary War there was a time of prosperity and improving economic conditions. We will see this later in the years following World Wars I and II.

"For the three years 1782, 1783 and 1784, following peace, conditions were fairly prosperous because of the reaction from the strain, the jubilant feeling of victory and as a result of war demands and the comparatively abundant *specie* (coin) left in the country by the British and French armies. But this was not to last long. The brief period of over-trading led to the depression of 1785 to 1789. The coin quickly left the country for payment of imported goods," according to Lightner. Industry and commerce were hampered by the absence of a good monetary system.

After the surge in activity which peaked in 1785 a decline came in prices which is the main element around which all else revolves in the long wave. America was a nation hardly three years old when we were introduced to the hard reality of the international power play of nation against nation in international commerce. Scarcely weaned, we were banned from trade in the British West Indies in 1784. Like a young couple living on love,

35

our young nation was elated by its new-found freedom. But the honeymoon was soon over and the bills had to be paid. American merchants found themselves embarrassed when they had no money to cover credit purchases from overseas. The government was forced to beg for loans from foreign governments. Perhaps in its scope and scale, this crisis was greater than the Great Depression, relatively speaking. Benjamin Franklin couldn't get the money he asked for from France because they were having problems as well.

Another interesting occurrence at this time was the first protective tariffs against foreign competition. This legacy haunts us today and plays an extremely important role in the cycle. It is important to point out that these tariffs came by the support of none other than the manufacturers without concern for the consumer — a tradition still kept today. Even with the tariffs, trade was surprisingly respectable.

An interesting note for our protectionist warlords of today is that America ran a trade deficit for 59 years after her freedom from England. The year 1840 was the first year we showed a surplus; the figures were $113,896,000 in exports and $107,142,000 in imports. We were insightful enough to see that profits made on the goods sold here were reloaned and reinvested in America. Maybe we could learn more than a few political lessons from our founding fathers.

These were trying times as European manufacturers, while selling their goods in America, were attempting to stifle start-up manufacturing in America. A humorous account records the ends to which the British were willing to go to secure their markets.

"In 1787 a Philadelphia man came into possession of two carding and spinning machines which were supposed to save the labor of 120 men a day. These machines were purchased by an agent of a British manufacturer and shipped back to Liverpool, the object being to nip American manufacturing in the bud," according to Lightner.

No doubt this is a comical story when considering the awesome force and world power the United States manufacturing sector has grown to be. We hear rumors today of Exxon buying up 200 mpg engines. Will we one day look back in comical relief from the 21st century as we scoot along in our electric cars seeing the humor only Father Time possesses?

The depression of 1785 brought on conditions that spawned our first insurrection in the form of Shay's Rebellion. This rebellion had 15,000 supporters. Being blessed with far more zeal than leadership, they were soon dispersed. Times were bad for our new nation, to say the least, but we were a nation with a vision and in 1791 we chartered the First Bank of the United States. The constitution had gone into effect in 1789 which had granted government the sole right to coin money and before long we were back in business. It was this time that marks the beginning rise in international prices that peaked in 1814. This period represents the first half of the first long-wave cycle.

American trade exploded in the early 1790s due to the war that broke out between France and England which the rest of Europe was soon drawn into.

"It was in this period that America was master of the seas so far as merchant-carrying trade was concerned. There was a large and steady demand for our agricultural products among the belligerent countries. Our foreign trade increased four fold in a decade," according to Lightner.

We had a recession in 1808 and 1809 due to an embargo by Jefferson. This embargo was created in response to Napoleon's decrees against neutral trade.

"In a single year our exports fell from $108,300,000 to $22,400,000 — far greater proportionately and much more abruptly than any cessation of business known in our history," according to Lightner.

Jefferson gave in to pressure and lifted the embargo and business soon returned. The year 1812 found us once again in war with England. Washington was captured by the British on August 24, 1814, sending shock waves through the financial markets. We rebounded quickly after the war which had been a humiliating draw at best even with our excellent showing at the Battle of New Orleans.

The rebound following the war did not last very long as the Napoleonic Wars had ended and Europe was in the midst of a severe depression. Europe began the decline of the long-wave cycle in 1815 and the United States followed suit in 1818.

"In 1818 the report became widespread that the banks were in critical condition. An attempt had been made to resume *specie* payment, but this had failed, being successful only in spots or for a limited time. In preparation for this the banks had restricted their loans, limiting credits to business and agriculture. The following year business felt the full effects of depression. In 1819 steps were taken to compel banks to pay *specie* or forfeit their charters. Many banks seeing this was impossible suspended, bringing the first widespread panic in our history," according to Lightner. So here we are witnessing what later emerges as the first decline of the long-wave cycle.

As we look at the history of decline it is important that we look at prices. Looking at the past 200 years we see prices flowing with the long-wave cycle in four distinct cycles. The forces at work in the long-wave cycle create the harmony between supply and demand. Let us take a quick look at what was happening throughout the world as we begin to see that prices cannot rise forever.

"During the four years between 1817 and 1821 the holders of property in the United States were supposed to have suffered a depreciation of nearly $800 million. General bankruptcy spread its darkness over the land; many of the wealthiest families were reduced to poverty; laborers suffered for want of bread; improvements of all sorts were abandoned and a scene of the most intense national distress ensued. As the tide of internal commerce had risen, there had been a general expansion of business. A depression had to come for several reasons: first, as a reflection of European troubles; second, a stoppage of overproduction; and third, to get money on a better basis," according to Lightner.

The comparison of the conditions of the 1810s with the 1980s are all too obvious as conditions right for a decline. Even with a clear understanding of the long-wave cycle, the similarities provide an eerie sensation.

We see a number of recessions on the way to the bottom of the first long-wave decline. The year 1825 saw the collapse of cotton prices in England and subsequently the collapse of banks in New Orleans. This crisis lasted only a few months and order was soon restored. A recession from 1837 to 1839 was due almost entirely to banking speculation and crop failures. We had a period of inflation that was brief and we then saw United States wholesale prices drop to their lowest points of the cycle in the early 1840s.

There was another recession in 1847 that was short-lived due to the discovery of gold in California which restored enthusiasm to all financial markets and confidence in general. The period between 1837 and 1857 is considered the "Golden Age" in United States history. This period covered the last 10 years of the decline of the first cycle as well as the first 10 years of the upswing of the second cycle. We were blessed with another recession in 1857. Some attributed this recession to the reduction of tariffs which flooded the country with imports. Others, a bit more attuned to the situation, saw other causes.

"There had been an enormous addition to the circulating medium of the country in the form of both gold and bank notes and speculation both in lands and industrial enterprises was rampant," wrote Lightner.

The Golden Age had seen enormous advances in the accumulation of wealth in this country which was accompanied by an increase in prices.

"During the period 1850 to 1857 President Buchanan calculated the production of gold in the United States at $400 million," Lightner wrote.

This same period had seen a doubling in banks in the country and the construction of railroads had seen an explosion as the U.S. had seven-ninths of the world's railroad milage.

"People apparently invested purely in their imagination of the future," according to Lightner.

There are incredible stories of the banking conditions during this time.

One account tells of a bank examiner as he traveled through the Midwest. The banks knew his travel plans and had the same gold coin follow him around to be whisked in the back door of the banks he visited and quickly deposited in the vault. There was a vast amount of fraud and circulation of bad notes.

"In the year 1858 Nichols' Bank Note Reporter carried 5,400 separate descriptions of false money," according to Lightner. "While admittedly the depression was due to underlying causes, such as speculation and overexpansion of credit, together with the unprecedented high prices occasioned by the enormous output of gold from California and Australia, it is generally accepted that a single incident pricked the bubble, as usual."

This account has a special ring to it as we consider the recent Ohio Savings and Loan episode.

"The story goes that the Ohio Life Insurance Company had $5 million tied up in railroad loans and their New York agent defaulted, causing the failure of the company with large liabilities. One institution after another followed suit, as did many of the eastern railroads. In 1857 there were almost 5,000 failures," according to Lightner.

This recession could be compared with the recession of 1974 in relation to the long wave. Surprisingly the resilience of the U.S. economy helped make a quick comeback from the recession in 1857 and by 1860 things were back to normal with business as well as prices on the rise in tune with the long-wave pattern.

The first half of the year 1860 saw business running as usual but as the election drew near the storm clouds began to form on the horizon. Business began to slow with heightened tensions in both the North and the South. November saw the election of Abraham Lincoln and "business stood breathlessly awaiting developments," wrote Lightner.

December 20, 1860 saw the secession of South Carolina from the Union which proved the beginning of wild confusion in financial markets.

"Bankers and financiers the country over perceived the gravity of the situation. They feared that the nation's trade would collapse and the whole framework of our political and financial system would be in danger," according to Lightner.

The lines were soon drawn and in 1861: "The South proceeded to repudiate its obligations to the North. The whole amount of southern indebtedness to the North was estimated by intelligent merchants in New York and Boston at $2 billion and a large part of it was lost at the breaking out of war," wrote Lightner. The year 1865 brought peace and the entire nation breathed "a sigh of relief," according to Lightner. Business in the North revived very quickly but the South was held responsible to repay many debts she had assumed to finance the war. The South was in deep depression for a number of years. She did revive a bit and the wheels of commerce began to roll as the preserved union re-entered the world market.

We saw a peak in U.S. prices in 1864 due to the war while European prices climbed until 1873. We will later see that after the long wave cycle peaks it plateaus for a number of years as the world economy is adjusting to the major shifts that create the long wave. This plateau has proven to be a prosperous period that leads to a peak in financial markets just before a major decline.

The late 1860s and early 1870s represent this plateau that we saw again in the 1920s and which we are currently witnessing in the 1980s.

We faced a small recession in 1869 due mainly to speculation in gold. September 24, 1869 was known as "Black Friday" due to the crash in the gold market. There were a number of failures during this time but the panic soon passed and business was back to normal. There had been a steady advance in the long wave since 1849 and we see it beginning to peak in the late 1860s with world prices at their highest points since 1815.

We will see later that the relations of nations during the 19th century were creating a global world economy that is beginning to be affected by the conditions of its particular participants. Expansion and contraction were beginning to be seen internationally and the affects were sobering.

With this in mind, we begin looking for comparisons of the conditions today and those of the past. Economic conditions seem to tell us that we reached another peak in the long wave in the early 1980s and are currently in the plateau period and heading for a crash. Looking back at the 1870s we see interesting comparisons.

"Every line of industry had been stimulated beyond its needs in anticipation of still greater profits. Borrowers went heavily into debt, paying high rates of interest, to develop new industrial enterprises with the inevitable consequences of overproduction. The depression of 1873 was marked by failures and bankruptcy of many banks and business houses all over the country. This was a worldwide depression. It began in Vienna in May, 1873, spreading through Europe, particularly to London and then to the United States. It affected Austria-Hungary, England, Germany, Italy, Russia and South America," according to Lightner.

In the United States there were over 20,000 business failures, money loss of a billion dollars and over three million men lost their jobs.

With the depression of 1873-78 came the beginning of the decline of the second long-wave cycle. Internationally, prices began to slide and did not reach their bottom until 1896. During this decline there were recessions of brief effect in 1878, 1884 and 1889. The years 1893 to 1895 brought a more acute recession that proved to be the force that bottomed the great cycle.

The industrialization of the world made this recession unusually difficult with large amounts of people being thrown out of work in industrialized regions. This brought on severely depressed conditions that would not have had as severe effects on a population that wasn't centralized for industrial output. During this time great industrial centers were emerging in the Northeast that were extremely vulnerable to recessions. But coming out of this setback, America and the world were in an advancing upswing of the long wave that would see the international marketplace reach such levels as were never dreamed possible.

International finance was seeing the dawn of a new era of growth and prosperity. Even World War I proved to slow the advance of the new world economy for only a short season. Of course the War had drastic effects on European industry but it revived fairly quickly.

The upswing of the third long wave was noted by a number of small recessions. A recession in 1903 was attributed to the monetary policy initiated in 1896. There was a large drop in stocks on all the exchanges but the industrial machinery of the Western world soon pulled us through and had us on the move again.

We suffered a slight financial panic in 1907 that brought about the passage of the Federal Reserve Act in an attempt to constrain speculation. With the outbreak of World War I in 1914, international financial markets were in confusion and every stock exchange in the world was closed. Financial markets soon regained stability yet business was hampered according to the nations that were at war with one another.

Large amounts of gold were recalled from the United States which were owed to Europe, but as we began to export war material the gold flowed back. The panic brought by the war caused a recession in the U.S. This recession was brief as orders began pouring in from Europe in 1915.

In 1920 we had a prelude of what was to come in 1929, as we entered into a fairly severe recession not terribly different from the recession in 1980. Prices dropped drastically in the first few years of the decade yet held their ground until 1929 when the bottom fell out of world prices. The United States had 50 percent of the world's gold in its vaults in 1920. This gave us the feeling of security. The recession of 1920 was marked by no runs on banks or major failures in the corporate community. Business slowed but was soon back to normal and was building steam as we moved through the roaring 20s with a vengeance.

The 1920s were the plateau period of which we have spoken and gave the illusion of a prospering period. There was virtually no inflation and in many areas there was deflation as we are seeing again today. The stock market was surging as overexpansion of industry left nowhere else for money to go. This is clearly another comparison with today. Interest rates were falling during the 20s just as we have seen in the 80s. Deregulation of financial and other industries was a great theme during the 20s and is a tune being played again in the 80s.

Agriculture was in a severe depression in the 20s just as we see today. Virtually every industry was fighting for protectionism in a world economy that was overproducing. The close observer saw many disturbing signs as the roaring 20s approached the close of a decade of good times.

Many theories surround the worldwide depression that began in 1929 and threw the world into a decade of industrial decline and stagnation. There are, however, a few realities accepted by everyone. Prices had begun to decline in 1920, which undermined industrial outlays and expansion. The entire economy was clearly overproducing. As companies realized they were pouring money into a bottomless hole by expanding in a deflating economy, they began to slow expansion in 1928. In June of 1929 industrial expansion, production and output peaked and began to decline. Corporate, personal and government debt had built up just as it had in the early 1870s. There was only one place for prices to go with no buying power behind industry or the individual. Stock markets had such momentum and speculative force that it was late October before the markets came to the realization that there was no economy underneath them to speak of.

I can't help but think of the roadrunner cartoon in which the coyote runs off the road and keeps running in mid-air for some time before he finally stops and looks down to realize he left solid ground some time back. At this point he proceeds to fall into a deep canyon.

The free fall that inevitably came in 1929 brought destruction to the world economy that could never have been imagined. Details of the stock market crash are fascinating. Many have the tendency to equate the depression with the crash but the crash was only a symptom of the underlying problem. The market crash and the depression would be comparable to an uncontrollable sneeze at the outset of pneumonia. The economy had taken its inevitable long-wave course and was to see a slowing of activity, not thinking to ask the permission of the stock market.

As the cycle continued its downward momentum the world banking order collapsed in 1933 and the world was taken off the gold standard. Unemployment reached as high as 25 percent of the working population in the United States as the industrial complex continued its demise. World trade was cut in half during the early 30s due to the foolish protectionism of the nations of the world who failed to see their great interdependence with one another. The Smoot-Hawley tariffs almost single-handedly wiped out world trade.

The growing strength of the world economy and the power wielded by bodies such as the Federal Reserve Board has tended to lengthen the advance of the long wave thus creating volatile markets in the last few years of the plateau as we saw in the 20s. This leads to an accelerated decline because of the height that debt and prices are able to reach.

This can be seen clearly as the early 80s saw the peak of the longest advance to date of the long-wave cycle. By allowing debt and prices to reach heights they couldn't in the first two cycles this longer advance naturally leads to an accelerated decline when it finally comes.

In the 1930s this accelerated decline brought about a premature bottom in the long-wave decline, thus bringing a premature beginning of the fourth advance. We will see this again in the mid- to late 90s with the beginning of the fifth cycle. The current heights of debt and prices are unprecedented and will lead to a sharp purifying decline. The outbreak of World War II also had an enormous impact on the beginning of the fourth cycle of the long wave.

It should be noted that the U.S. had a setback in 1937-38 as she began working her way out of the depression. The seriousness and depth of the third long-wave decline came as the great depression. The great depression is attributed to isolationism in world markets and a hesitancy of the business community in the fear and memory of what we had just been through.

World War II helped put the memory of the depression out of our minds as we went to work to defeat the Nazi war machine.

Following the war there was a definite decline in output beginning in March 1945, but by November things picked up and the economy was on the rebound. We saw another slight setback in 1948, but the long wave was moving up and we soon pulled out of it. We saw slight recessions in 1958 and 1961 but these were soon forgotten as the economy continued to expand in the upswing.

The height of our involvement in Vietnam brought recession in 1968 because of the large drain on our national resources as well as being a time of national worry and frustration.

The year 1973 gave us the energy crisis as well as a business recession followed by exploding prices. Of course 1981 was our most recent business downturn as supply-side economics took initial effect.

We now find ourselves in a period very comparable to the

1920s as we hear cries for government to get off the backs of the people and deregulation is the theme of the day. We saw a peak in prices in the early 80s just as we saw in 1920. This is a time of cautious expansion and capital outlays as the keen observer sees an erosion of real prices under the surface and the potential for a crash in world prices brought on by falling oil prices.

It is clear that prices for raw materials and commodities peaked from 1980 to 1981. The fourth advance of the long-wave began around 1939 to 1940 and peaked, as far as real capital expansion, in 1980 to 1981, just as the third cycle peaked in 1920 to 1921. We are fast approaching the edge of the fourth plateau of the long-wave cycle. The signs are evident as the equity markets are in euphoria with the illusion of a strong world economy where inflation is a thing of the past. It is time someone take a close look and see what the facts are telling us and what really lies ahead.

This chapter has been an effort to give an overview, if ever so shallow, of the time period we will be looking at to develop and apply long-wave theory.

Chapter Three will introduce you to the man who first observed the long wave and the conclusions he came to. The cycle does not have to be as severe as it has been in the past. The leaders of the world are at fault for not acknowledging the natural laws that guide the cycle.

The Great Depression was the result of man attempting to force the economy in the opposite direction the long wave was attempting to carry it. The long wave can be distorted for a season but in the long run, nature always wins. We can either learn from our mistakes or we can forget the pain felt by previous generations.

It is my fear that the leaders of the the world economy will not recognize the familiar storm on the horizon and the inevitable passing of the economic seasons. As a result the whole world will suffer. Intermediate planning is not always enough for long-range goals and if history is our teacher it is highly probable the wrong moves will be made and the coming decline will be far worse than it has to be.

But for the investor, just as appropriate clothing protects from the winter, so certain investment instruments protect from the cycle. Long-range planning is not for the near-sighted investor. Long-range planning is for the investor with patience and a sincere belief in the reality that history repeats itself.

3

A Forgotten Russian

From the heart of Russia in 1892 came the life of one Ni-kolai Dmitryevitch Kondratieff. He grew up during the turmoil of the fall of the Russian monarchy and the emergence of a to-talitarian dictatorship. His interests were turned towards eco-nomics which proved to be his livelihood as well as the cause of his premature death. He was a member of the left-wing Socialist Revolutionary party from 1917 to 1919.

Kondratieff was active director of an institute of economics in Moscow from 1920 to 1928 where his interest turned from Soviet planning, in which he worked to develop the first five-year agricultural plan, to the more fascinating analysis of the rise and fall of the capitalist system. His new interest did not sit well with the Stalin regime, nor did his struggle for more agricultural independence in the Soviet system. Kondratieff was rewarded in the usual Stalin style with his arrest and imprison-ment in a slave-labor camp.

Alexander Solzhenitsyn, in his book, *The Gulag Archipela-go,* told of the horrible death Kondratieff suffered in a cold dark cell of solitary confinement in a prison camp located deep in the wilderness of Russia's Siberia. His death came only after the fulfillment of his prophecy of the inevitable downturn of the third cycle of his research. The third downturn came as the Great Depression.

As Kondratieff looked over and studied 140 years of histo-ry in the free-market system and the economy of the world, he saw something quite different from what his peers and predeces-sors had seen. Perhaps it was an accident and most surely it took him by surprise. As most economists of his day as well as to-day, Kondratieff had limited his vision and study and had never stepped back and taken in a sweeping, all-encompassing view of economic history.

But somewhere between 1919 and 1921 Kondratieff saw

emerging from prices, interest rates, production and human nature the rise and fall of the long-wave cycle. History has shown that most prophets are rejected in their native land. Nikolai Kondratieff proved to be no exception to this rule. Stalin enjoyed the idea of the eventual collapse of the free world's economy but he was furious with Kondratieff's finding that the free market would come back stronger than ever after being purged of its inefficiencies.

Kondratieff wrote of two and a half long-wave cycles, the first beginning in a trough (economic low-point) in 1789 and peaking in 1814, then declining to its completion in 1849. He wrote of a plateau period that followed the peak in the cycle which lasts seven to 10 years as the economy adjusts to the great changes it is going through. The notion of a plateau should be taken literally.

To gain a clear understanding of the long-wave plateau you should picture in your mind a geographical plateau. You have a steep and lengthy climb to the top of a plateau. The top of the plateau is a level area that brings stability for a time. But after crossing the plateau you come to the edge where you face the inevitable steep drop and decline from the plateau. The economy builds up and expands through the years with rising prices and increasing debt climbing to great heights of output, production and efficiency. After moving through great advances and expansion the economy has outdone itself, quite literally. The economy then levels off as it tries to adjust. This is the plateau.

It would be nice if we could stay at these lofty heights forever. The problem is that the economy has gone too far and is producing too many goods in every area. With too many companies producing too much you start to see falling prices. This is what happened in 1920 and 1980 as both these dates mark our entrance into the plateau of the long wave.

Falling prices are first welcomed after coming through a period of inflation. During the plateau there is the illusion that the economy is improving and becoming very stable. The plateau is really only one last Indian summer boom before the bust. The market is flooded with cash during the plateau because there is nowhere for money to go. Every area of the economy has been stimulated beyond the world's true needs and demands. Because of the great amounts of cash with no place to go, the plateau always sees booming stock markets throughout the world. Lower interest rates, deflationary pressures and slowed outlays all have the effect of freeing cash for the stock markets.

The second cycle began its upswing in 1849 and plateaued from the late 60s to the mid-70s where it began its decline to its bottom in 1896.

The third cycle began its climb in 1896, peaked in 1920, plateaued through the 20s and began its rapid decline in 1929. Kondratieff acknowledged that the dates of turning and peaks are flexible, give or take a few years and are not intended to be dogmatically and rigidly interpreted. His work was published in 1926 and so it did not record the cycle's full plateau through the decade of the 20s and the drastic crash in the early 30s.

The advance of the fourth cycle was begun by the enormous war effort in all industrial nations in the late 30s and early 40s. The fourth cycle was able to start fairly early because of a premature bottom of the third decline. This was due to the severity of the great crash that came fast and hard and thus effectively purged the economy of its inefficiencies. It is true that without the war the cycle could well have started in the mid- to late 40s but this is only a guess. The force and effect of war on the economy must be realized as an all-important element in the cycle.

We discussed briefly in Chapter Two what I believe to be emerging as a new era in the long-wave cycle. Kondratieff was unable to see this because of its uniqueness to this century and the fact that his data only covered through the early 1920s. This new era in the long wave is creating a more lengthy advance of approximately 50 years and a sharper decline of five to 10 years. This is due to the new interrelationship of the world economy which allows debt and prices to reach enormous heights.

Because the free-world economy is so tightly bound together by the ever-growing strength of the world marketplace we are able to hold together far longer than in the past before we eventually collapse.

The emerging world marketplace allows the world economy to expand further and reach far greater heights than nations reached independently during past cycles. Our world economy and close associations cannot stop the inevitable but only postpone it.

The height that debt, prices and expansion are able to reach today will produce a faster decline that will clean inefficiency and stagnation out of the system far quicker than in past cycles. The evidence is clear that the fourth long-wave advance started in the late 30s and we entered the plateau in the early 80s. We are once again on the plateau that Kondratieff wrote of and we are fast approaching a major decline and collapse.

I believe it is very important to take a close look at what the father of long-wave cycle theory had to say. This chapter is dedicated to what Kondratieff discovered, believed and wrote.

Kondratieff reinforced the belief that the dynamics of free-market economies are not linear (in a straight line) and continually progressing upward. Kondratieff clearly saw the world economy as cyclical (in cycles) in nature. He acknowledged that each cycle advanced and developed the economy further and brought it to new heights, but clearly taught that the advance was a cyclical advance and not a linear advance.

He taught and believed in the intermediate seven-to-11-year cycle that many teach today. However, Kondratieff taught that reducing the system to this intermediate cycle was simplistic and that a broader scope should be superimposed onto the system that has a cycle average of 50 or so years. He recognized and was open to the necessity of flexibility in the system and said, "the long cycle fluctuates between 45 and 60 years which is to say 25 percent."

Here he pointed out as well the flexibility of the intermediate cycle or the seven-to-11-year cycle is a greater 57 percent. Another cycle accepted today and recognized by Kondratieff is based on the work of Kichen who showed a three-and-one-half-to-four-and-one-half-year cycle within the intermediate cycle.

The foundation to Kondratieff's theory and the element I consider to be most important in evaluating the long-wave cycle is prices. Wholesale and commodity (basic goods: wheat, oil, pork bellies, etc.) prices have followed closely the outline Kondratieff laid out in the rise and fall of the long wave. The graphs included show the French, English and United States commodity prices used by Kondratieff in his research. Retail prices are not subject to following the cycle as closely as wholesale and commodity prices but remain higher which is in part what precipitates and causes the collapse. We are all aware of the enormous decline in prices at the beginning of the great depression and the beginning rise in prices at the outset of World War II.

Prices have continued to rise until the early 80s where we have seen a decline in many prices and slowed increases across the board. We have seen a slide in the price of almost all commodities in the past few years. This should be raising a danger sign that we are once again in a long-wave plateau.

Oil began a rapid decline in the early 80s and is at risk of a

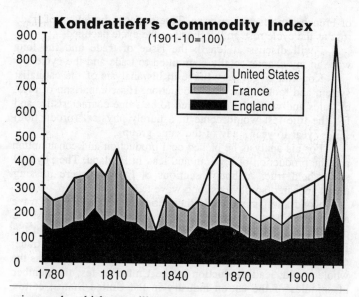

Kondratieff's Commodity Index
(1901-10=100)

price crash, which we will see later is the wild card in our next decline or potential crash.

Many agricultural prices have fallen by more than 50 percent since 1980. We cannot over-emphasize the fact that Kondratieff taught the long wave peaked and then plateaued for a number of years before going into its decline.

The 80s, like the 20s, represent the plateau period of the long wave which, due to the forces at work, are seeing falling real prices and soaring stock markets. This is happening while debt is still on the rise — as it was in the 20s.

Could we really be on a plateau that is with every passing day bringing us closer and closer to the edge of a collapse? I believe this is the exact scenario we are indeed facing and the evidence to support this hypothesis is very convincing. We are all aware that a price collapse in every sector of the world economy would bring the stock markets crashing and all expansion to a halt. The incredible amounts of debt throughout every area of the economy will only magnify the collapse.

Moving on into Kondratieff's research we find he brings wages and trade into the long wave. Kondratieff analyzed the weekly levels of wages in the English cotton and textile industry as well as the number of agricultural workers. To look at trade's relation to the long wave Kondratieff observed the sum of French exports and imports. True to form the levels of trade rose as the cycle rose and declined as the cycle declined.

I will discuss at length the issue of trade and the long wave in my chapter totally committed to trade and the cycle.

Kondratieff got very brave in his analysis of the capitalist system and took a look into production. His comparison of prices, rates and wages he considered to be value characteristics and felt the true test would come in a purely physical (production) series (year to year study of the same group).

For his analysis he picked coal production and consumption and the production of pig iron and lead in England. The physical series held true. Although sections of the data were missing there appeared an obvious long-wave trend.

Kondratieff mentioned other series in which the long wave appeared evident. A number of such series were as follows: the deposits and the portfolio of the bank of France; deposits at the French banks; English imports and total English foreign trade; coal production in the United States and Germany, as well as the whole world; lead production in the United States; the number of spindles of the cotton industry in the United States; cotton acreage in the United States; and oat acreage in France.

A major reason for Kondratieff's conclusions on the long wave come from the historical rise and fall of interest rates. He believed analysis of interest rates should be based on yields from government bonds because of their stability relative to other instruments, so he looked at yields and prices from the French *rente* and the English *consol* (both are government bonds). True to form the price of bonds follow a long-wave cycle.

Although Kondratieff did not use the United States' yields and prices, they follow closely the French and English model. Interest rates reach their peaks as the long-wave cycle peaks and decline as the cycle declines. Prices of bonds reach their lows during the peak of the long wave and reach their highs during the trough of the long wave. Of course interest rates have a direct impact on economic activity and the expansion of all sectors of the economy. High rates bring less capital expansion so business activity begins to slow in the peak.

It should be noted that the peak in bond yields and their lowest prices come as the economy enters the plateau period which is a number of years before the peak in the stock markets.

Chapter 14 will take a more in-depth look at bonds and their relation to the long wave.

In observing the fluctuation of rates Kondratieff remarked,

"The periods of these cycles agree rather closely with the corresponding periods in the movements of wholesale commodity prices."

In review of his statistical findings, Kondratieff made the following observations which I quote from his interpreted article, "The Long Waves In Economic Life," that was republished in *Readings in Business Cycle Theory* in 1951.

> *(1) The movements of the series which we have examined running from the end of the 18th century to the present time show long cycles. Although the statistical-mathematical treatment of the series selected is rather complicated, the cycles discovered cannot be regarded as the accidental result of the methods employed. Against such an interpretation is to be set the fact that these waves have been shown with about the same timing in all the more important of the series examined.*
>
> *(2) The cycles accelerate or retard the rate of growth in series that don't show a trend.*
>
> *(3) There is a very close correspondence in the timing of the wave movements of the series in the individual countries, in spite of the difficulties present in the treatment of these data. Deviations from the general rule that prevail in the sequence of the cycles are very rare.*
>
> *(4) The method according to which the statistical data have been analyzed permits an error of five to seven years in the determination of the years of such turnings.*
>
> *(5) Naturally, the fact that the movement of the series examined runs in long cycles does not yet prove that such cycles also dominate the movement of all other series. Our investigation has also extended to series in which no waves were evident. On the other hand, it is by no means essential that the long waves embrace all series.*
>
> *(6) The long waves we have established relative to the series most important in economic life are international; and the timing of these cycles corresponds fairly well for European capitalistic countries. On the basis of the data that we have adduced, we can venture the statement that the same timing holds also for the United States.*

After Kondratieff had exhausted his statistical studies of the long-wave cycle, he began to look at the empirical (practical, non-scientific) characteristics of the rise and fall in capitalist countries.

He introduced this area of his study with the following statement: "From another point of view, the historical material relating to the development of economic and social life as a whole confirms the hypothesis of long waves. Several general propositions which we have arrived at concerning the existence and importance of long waves are as follows."

These are again direct quotations:

> *(1) The long waves belong really to the same complex dynamic process in which the intermediate cycles of the capitalistic economy with their principal phases of upswing and depression run their course. These intermediate cycles, however, secure a certain stamp from the very existence of the long waves. Our investigation demonstrates that during the rise of the long waves, years of prosperity are more numerous, whereas years of depression predominate during the downswing.*

> *(2) During the recession of the long waves, agriculture, as a rule, suffers especially pronounced and long depression. This was what happened after the Napoleonic Wars; it happened again from the beginning of the 1870s onward; and the same can be observed in the years after World War I.*

> *(3) During the recession of the long waves, an especially large number of important discoveries and inventions in the technique of production and communication are made, which, however, are usually applied on a large scale only at the beginning of the next long upswing.*

> *(4) At the beginning of a long upswing, gold production increases as a rule and the world market for goods is generally enlarged.*

> *(5) It is during the period of the rise of the long waves, i.e., during the period of high tension in the expansion of economic forces, that, as a rule, the most disastrous and extensive wars and revolutions occur.*

Kondratieff concluded, "It is to be emphasized that we attribute to these recurring relationships an empirical character only, and that we do not by any means hold that they contain the explanation of the long waves."

In Kondratieff's discussions on the nature of long waves he emphasized the relationship of gold to the cycle. He realized that gold is a commodity and has a cost of production. Once the economy has moved into the decline the cost of production is at a low point. There is naturally going to be more gold production because gold will have its greatest purchasing power at the time of its being cheapest to produce.

Because of the complexity of gold and its pricing in a volatile economy I will spend an entire chapter discussing gold's relation to the cycle — especially the coming downturn.

Kondratieff's conclusions in his presentation on the long wave emphasize his increasing conviction of its existence while at the same time hinting of the question as to its origin: "The objections to the regular cyclical character of the long waves, therefore, seem to be unconvincing. We believe ourselves justified in saying that the long waves, if existent at all, are a very important and essential factor in economic development, a factor the effects of which can be found in all the principal fields of social and economic life. Even granting the existence of long waves, one is, of course, not justified in believing that economic dynamics consist only in fluctuations around a certain level. The course of economic activity represents beyond doubt a process of development, but this development obviously proceeds not only through intermediate waves but also through long ones. In alerting the existence of long waves and in denying that they arise out of random causes, we are also of the opinion that the long waves arise out of causes which are inherent in the essence of the capitalistic economy. This naturally leads to the question as to the nature of these causes."

I agree emphatically with Kondratieff that the causes of the long wave are inherent within the free-market system. I am of the inclination that this is not a flaw within the system. The long wave is part of the unique beauty and challenge of the system and is the free market's way of cleaning out the impurities that have built up. The build-up of debt and the overly speculative spirit as well as overproduction and inflation have to be purged from the system for it to get a fresh start. The economy is purified and purged by the long-wave cycle.

Someone will invariably say, "Kondratieff wrote this theory in 1926; this is the 1980s, age of the microchip and monetary control. Surely you don't think we will ever see the second half or collapse of the fourth cycle?"

The cycle of which Kondratieff wrote and the cycle I am convinced exists is beyond the reach of innovation and monetary control. No more than a meteorologist can control the path of a hurricane can the Federal Reserve, the World Bank or anyone else control the inevitable downturn that is closing in upon us.

Weather satellites are the highest technology in the prediction of hurricanes, but do they prevent the coast from being smashed by high winds and waves?

The answer is, of course, no, but there is a lesson to be learned here. The satellite, if heeded, can save valuable property and possession and needless loss and pain. The closeness of the

analogy hits home in the idea of heading for safer ground. The
digital readouts and computer displays of our high tech economy
are warning of a hurricane just out to sea. Their is certainly safe
ground for you and your investments, but timing is crucial.

The Federal Reserve can lessen the impact with intelligent
decision making but they cannot change the inevitable. We have
already witnessed a full cycle since Kondratieff published his
work; in fact, 1986 marked the 60th anniversary of the publishing of his findings.

We all tend to shun bad news and act as if it does not exist, especially during the day of plenty. Anyone who speaks of
bad times to come is avoided and disbelieved. However, these are
the ones who could smile in the early 30s watching their lot increase, while those who were enjoying the good life a few years
earlier were scrambling to save the devalued remains of their
lifelong investments. We are all aware of the advances and prosperity since the late 30s.

Perhaps it is time to take a close look at where we are and
what the future holds. Who in the mainstream of business today
can remember the pain of the past decline? Few, if any. There is
a new generation of optimists and risk-takers that is fueling this
economy with no recollection of the last decline and no perception of the waterfall that lies just around the next bend in the
river.

One is accurate in saying that today is extremely different
from the day of Kondratieff; indeed it is. But where do these
differences come and are they deep differences in the structure of
the economic system or are they only cosmetic differences that
cover the same old long-wave face?

4

The World Economy

The close of the 18th century, as Kondratieff has shown, saw the emergence of the international economic long-wave cycle. A new view of the economic world was also beginning to take shape and emerge at this time.

This view has gathered momentum over the past 200 years acquiring new strength over the past few years as we have seen international ownership and foreign investments exploding to record heights. This view is one of a world economy. Political ideology and government policy are as diverse today as they were 200 years ago. We have socialism, totalitarian dictatorships, military *juntas,* a few monarchies and varying strains of democratic states.

But no matter what the political style and belief, we all come together and eat from the same international economic table. We have no choice in the realm of international trade but to pay our bills in cash, secure a line of credit or dip into the till at the International Monetary Fund.

The world economy operates by accounting standards; governments may rise and fall but the business records are still being kept. To play in the international economic arena as a sovereign state, you must play by the rules.

There are a number of obvious forces at work that have shaped the emergence of a world economy over the past 200 years. A major player has been innovation in transportation. Shipping has evolved from often-unseaworthy sailing ships to vessels carrying vast amounts of goods to virtually any place in the world. Canals from the Suez to Panama have opened up trade lanes for enhanced efficiencies in international commerce. Railroads were on the cutting edge of the industrialization of the world as they brought the trade of the continents to the major world ports.

From Hong Kong to New York, from Bombay to Rotter-

dam and from Rio de Janeiro to Cape Town, the states and continents of the world were becoming interdependent on each other
for the flow of goods. Water transportation became more dependable for tourist and official travelers alike. Air travel began
to take off early in the 20th century and made the world even
more susceptible to international economic dealings.

Charles A. Lindbergh made history by flying across the
Atlantic from New York to Paris in 1927. This marked the beginning of a great explosion in business alliances between Europe and America. Air travel has been a major element in the advance of the world economy. If one element in the evaluation of
this New world economy could be placed on a pedestal, it
would perhaps be the advance by leaps and bounds in communications. In scarcely a century, the economic centers of the world
went from communication by pigeons to instantaneous communication and information by satellite. The impact at times is almost overpowering and unimaginable.

President Reagan takes a bullet from a would-be assassin's
gun in 1981 and within minutes we see the dollar fall to longtime lows on the major money exchanges from New York to
London to Tokyo. Half a millennium earlier America was not
even known to exist and England was still looking over her
shoulder for an invasion from barbarians.

One example of this new-world economy is that there is a
great deal of serious talk today about 24-hour trading on both
equity (stock) and money markets. This will make our financial
world seem even smaller. Imagine going to bed at 11 p.m. and
getting up at 6 a.m. to find the value of your portfolio to have
dropped by 25 percent. Speak of nightmares!

Through market linkage we will be able to buy shares of
Honda and Toyota as easily as Ford or GM. The NASDAQ (National Association of Securities Dealers and Automated Quotations) has seen explosive growth in recent years and is just recently beginning to challenge the Big Board in volume trades on
a daily basis. The New York Exchange still trades on an auction
basis whereas the NASDAQ is all based on computer trading.

Gordon S. Macklin, former NASDAQ president, has a
number of fascinating insights into coming changes to world
stock markets due to communications advances. Here are a few
remarks he made in a New York City speech in the fall of 1985:

> *Technology is making possible the international quota-*
> *tion, execution and clearing linkages for the world stock mar-*
> *ket of tomorrow. The large international securities firms —*

the Merrill Lynches, the Nomuras, the Shearson Lehmans, the Goldman Sachses, the Dean Witters, the Grieveson Grants and Morgan Grenfells, the Credit Suisse and First Bostons and others — all are building in-house systems that will allow them to participate fully in these emerging international linkages ... Private vendor organizations will play a crucial part in getting price information from the various markets and market makers to the end users — the world securities firms ... The vendors are betting that there will be a rapidly growing market for international quotation information. This is shown by the fact that AP, Dow Jones and Quotron, the largest domestic United States vendors, have launched a joint venture in Europe ...

There will be increasing pressure on the markets — London, NASDAQ, the continental European markets and, very importantly, Tokyo, the second-largest market in the world — to make ever more quotations available to each other and to the vendors and their subscribers. A world NASDAQ type price quotation network will be the first technological building block of the world stock market. As the quotation network grows, actual trading information will follow. NASDAQ was originally only a quotation-information system; today it receives and transmits last-sale information on more than 2,100 NASDAQ National Market System securities. The same development may be expected to follow in linked international markets ...

Merrill has been trading NASDAQ stocks around the clock for some time. The firm passes its book around the world, from New York to Tokyo to London and back to New York. It does the same thing for debt security trading in European and United States CD's commercial paper and bonds. Among foreign equities, Merrill trades Japanese, Amsterdam, Singapore and Hong Kong stocks on a 24-hour basis. For other foreign equities, one book moves from Johannesburg to London to New York ...

As the experience of firms also indicates, some customers want to deal at all hours, but generally more and more customers want to deal during their normal business hours. The push for the 24-hour world market is on. In a sense, there will not be a true world market until trading is continuous, around the clock.

There is no doubt many will fight such innovations but with terminals and phones at home, the office and in the car the brokerage community will soon adjust. News that affects the market is known immediately throughout the world due to our advances in communications. Advances in communications have done a great deal to increase banking transactions on an international basis which does a great deal to stimulate world trade. International orders are being processed in a fraction of the time it use to take because of the financial links through new communications technologies. Electronic transfer allows for same-day order execution from virtually any two locations in the world. There is no argument that communications have gone far to build our world economy.

Another all-important piece in the world economic puzzle was the rise of the international bankers late in the 18th century. The study of the rise of the banking families is fascinating. Before this new era, nations were as a rule financed from within for their various and sundry activities, whether public works or military conquest.

The international banking community emerged as a sovereign nation in and of itself, able to make or break leaders and guide the destinies of whole peoples by a simple yes or no in the request for financing by governments. Trade and commerce are financed through the network of the international bankers as well. Growth and stability can be controlled by their manipulation or influence on rates. Though divine right as a political institution faded during this time, we can still trace the linage within the world bankers today back to the original families of the international moneychangers of the 18th century. As we see the evolution of our world economic organism unfolding, we must label the international bankers and their operations as the blood that flows through the veins of the system, controlling the life of the entire entity.

Another element that is gaining strength with every passing day in our perception of the world organism is the multinational corporation. Many of these giants have a gross national product larger than dozens of our smaller nations' totalled together. They command vast empires on which the sun never sets. We tend to see control of the multinational residing in one nation but these companies are owned by residents of almost every nation in the world. No longer is GM held strictly by Americans who consider what is good for GM is good for America. This is causing the world to be tied together even more tightly in today's economy.

National companies that have chosen not to join the international trend must of necessity pay close attention to the rest of the world and what the competition on the other side is up to. In a general sense there is no longer such a thing as a domestic economy. You would be hard pressed to find any company that is not in some way affected by the world economy. The multinational has, perhaps more than any other element, brought government into our world organism.

Having a formidable interest in every corner of the world, the large multinational must have a vehicle to express its interest, needs and desires. Its tool and vehicle has inevitably fallen to the lot of government. It has even been rumored that governments have been toppled in line with the desires of the multinationals. They form a network in world commerce that tightens the bonds of the world economy.

Energy needs have come hand in hand with industrialization, so treaties and pacts between and among nations began to emerge. Alliances and trading partnerships were formed from every corner of the world. Certain regions had an abundance of energy but no climate for agriculture, so marriages were made and strategic interests were solidified by the fate of nature.

Looking at the past 20 years, there has been an enormous increase in foreign investment and ownership. Taking a close look at the United States model, we see total foreign assets in the United States rising from just over $100 billion in 1970 to around $1 trillion in 1985. The three major components of this investment are in treasury securities, direct investment and corporate stocks. High yields in the United States relative to other nations have been a big attraction; the United States is perceived as a safe haven as well as politically stable.

Agriculture is an all-important element in the rise of the world economy. The superfarm is changing the way the world feeds itself and is making many nations vulnerable to a healthy climate of world trade.

Western Europe is a slave to the oil fields of the volatile Middle East. Another example of interdependence in the world community is South Africa. As the major producer of a number of strategic metals used in the United States defense complex, the Pentagon watches closely the situation in a small nation thousands of miles away.

Before the 19th century, what happened in one country or region didn't have a very large impact on what went on in neighboring states. One nation could have been in economic turmoil and her neighbors may not even have known of her plight. The tulip fiasco in Holland in 1635 didn't have much of an effect on market conditions in London. Portugal's loss of a major trade expedition to hurricanes didn't affect the markets in Frankfurt,

Germany in 1675. Large public investments on the part of China in the Great Wall had no repercussions on Barbarian trade in Europe. Nations were independent economic entities or economic organisms that could get sick or die off without a large impact on the rest of the world.

The days of the lone nation are over. The independent organisms of nation states have evolved into a single living, breathing and seasonal organism that is today's world economy.

The depth to this new international relationship was shown clearly by Kondratieff's studies in the long wave. As pointed out in this chapter, transportation, communications, international banking, the multinational corporation, agriculture and foreign investments are all powerful elements that form the ups and downs of the long-wave cycle.

We again go back to observing the masterpiece and must force ourselves to step back and take in the entire international spectrum as we look at this world economic organism that reveals itself in the long-wave cycle. Could it be that the sum total of the components of the world economy is the force that guides the expansion and contraction of the long-wave cycle?

The reality of our current situation in a world economy brings us to a number of sobering conclusions. There is no such a creature as an independent sovereign economic nation. We are all bound by the world economy, thus our fate is linked by the system we are all a part of.

A small Third World nation can send shock waves through the world financial markets by its incapacity to pay its creditors. An oil tanker struck in the Persian Gulf in regional hostilities can send oil prices up on world markets. Above all, the downturn in a few nations can bring the entire world to its knees as we saw in the early 30s.

Of course, this works both ways and we have for the past 45 years seen an advancing world economy. The question arises: Are we now facing another fall in world prices and the inevitable effects such a fall would bring? In evaluating the situation we come to a simple yet telling conclusion: we are all in this thing together.

5

The Cycle and Psychology

What are we to make of the current world affair with *laissez-faire* economics, the supremacy of individual capitalism and the age of the entrepreneur?

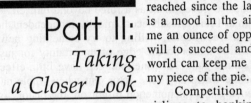

Optimism and the quest for the Almighty Dollar are at levels unreached since the late 1920s. There is a mood in the air that says give me an ounce of opportunity and the will to succeed and nothing in the world can keep me from cutting out my piece of the pie.

Competition is king. From airlines to banking to trucking, government is cutting the strings and letting the capitalist nature take its course. Conservative politics have long been the ticket of the free market and have endorsed the belief that the private sector can do far more to make society and the economy reach new heights of return and personal reward than can government. Indeed they are right, but what is the other side of the coin? For each action there is an equal and opposite reaction. Could it be possible that the psychology of man plays a role and is a large part of the rise and the fall of the long-wave cycle? The evidence leans towards just such a hypothesis.

Due to the amount of data available and the fact that the decline known as the Great Depression occurred in the 20th century, it is weighted heavily in our analysis of psychological implications of the long wave.

Though we can trace liberal and conservative political and social movements running in conjuncture with the long wave for the past 200 years, the Great Depression tells us far more about what to expect in the coming decline because of its closer approximation and resemblance to current times.

No doubt there are few who remember the pain of the depression in the 1930s. The yuppie generation of today has the perception of a fairly pain-free, riskless society; and they are the engine that is driving the new breed of speculators and risk-takers in today's markets. I have long enjoyed the political philosophy of Englishman Jeremy Bentham, who is quoted by Dick Stoken in an article on the Kondratieff Cycle and its effects on social psychology in the February 1980 issue of *The Futurist*.

Bentham said, "Nature has placed man under the governance of two sovereign masters, pain and pleasure. It is for them alone to point out what we shall do."

This thought conjures in me the vision of man as a great pendulum swinging back and forth within the economic long wave. Man first finds his economic freedom and taking it to a painful extreme he swings back to a stifling protectionist stance turning control back to government as a force beyond himself.

When one man finds himself economically independent he tends to become a freewheeler, willing to try something new, willing to step a little closer to the edge of uncertainty for just a little more economic gain. This one man can have little effect on the history of the world as a lone actor, but when whole nations are experiencing this phenomenon in unison, the history of humanity is hanging in the balance.

Fifty years is sufficient time to drain pessimistic and cautious blood out of the mainstream of economic activity. We tend to forget the stories our parents and grandparents told us of food and unemployment lines. Visions of the Great Depression are not real in the consciousness of those in a position to see it coming again and they take no action to lessen the impact.

Quoting Stoken: "When people perceive less risk they put more trust in their own powers. They become more adventurous and more willing to take chances. Because they are now being directed by a different set of underlying assumptions than during a downswing, they do things they would not have done during hard times. Economic success leads people to believe they now have control over their own destiny, with the power to solve their own and society's problems. They idealize existence and become less tolerant of injustice."

As the cycle peaks and begins its decline, the world takes on a new character and man is not so confident in his ability and power. Capitalism loses its luster and falls from its pedestal. Dreams and aspirations of the proponents of a *laissez-faire* system, being shattered, provide the pain necessary to begin the swing of the pendulum back to a sedated view of the system.

Quoting Stoken again: "On the one hand, a long period of prosperity and affluence produces increases in assets, wages, social mobility and the standard of living that exceed people's expectations, causing them to be pleasantly surprised. A depression on the other hand, has an unforward effect on jobs, wages and asset values. People unexpectedly see their goals frustrated and this serves as a lesson of pain. Pain produces a definite psychological change in most people. They become motivated to avoid pain and to seek security. In a risky world people feel helpless, lose faith in their own powers and become very cautious and unwilling to take chances. To protect themselves and ward off danger, they bond together into groups. To modify behavior in the direction of group unity, there must be rules and social restraints as well as the acceptance of some kind of authority. Naturally the mood at such a time runs against individualistic capitalism, with its free markets and emphasis on competition."

We can see this clearly in the growth of the unions in the 40s and the 50s as the pain of the depression was fresh on the minds of people all over the world, yet now as this generation has grown old and the economy is in good shape, we see unions struggling for survival. If history holds true, unions will once again be on the rise and membership will be booming soon after the world economy slides into another decline.

As the new-cautious and risk-averse generation begins to grow old and fresh blood comes into the system, there is a slow change occurring: a few individuals are stepping out from the group and bucking the trend. They are the inventors and the innovators that are, through their bold and aggressive natures, going to lead the world out of its mesmerized risk-averse state of decline and into the next advance of the long-wave cycle.

Chapter 10 is dedicated to the impact on the cycle of these men, their inventions and the technology of the day.

Currently we find everyone and his brother jumping on the entrepreneurial bandwagon as everything is looking up and everyone is prospering in an advancing economy. A large majority of these are parasites looking for a quick buck at the expense of someone else. The true entrepreneur emerges when the chips are down and the economy is in a decline. These are the entrepreneurs who have the "right stuff"; the imposters will be flushed out with the downturn.

There is a unique inversion that takes place in the long-wave cycle that is truly fascinating. During the upswing and long-wave advance, political and economic conservatism is pushing towards less government and more competitive *laissez-faire* economics, but at the same time we have a surge in social liberalism. The opposite occurs during the downswing and long-wave decline. We have politics embracing liberal ideology during the decline and taking power away from the people. Economically we see a turn from *laissez-faire* policies to more government control and intervention. But socially we see a revival in conservative ways of thinking as traditional values make a comeback.

In the upswing moral and ethical restraints are being cast off for more permissive and rebellious attitudes. Discipline and authority are lost concepts and the younger generation grows up with a carefree, easy-come, easy-go attitude to the frustration of parents who worked hard for their place in society.

Perhaps herein lies a clue to the imminent demise of the economy. For this generation has a misconception of hard work and the value of a hard-earned dollar. Good economic instincts are learned — not hereditary. While the parents of this new generation were working to provide their children with something more of the good life, the children's value systems became distorted and meaningless. Yet these children have grown up to be the managers of today. Their way of looking at the world, as if it owes them, is unique within the peak of the long-wave cycle.

As the world economy begins to decline, conservative politics take a back seat to sweeping liberal political plans and government's re-involvement in the private sector.

Herbert Hoover was defeated in the 1932 elections and with him went conservative politics. Hoover did not lose by as large a margin as many believe and it would be possible for a conservative Republican to be reelected if he had the right appeal. Because the nation and world will be experiencing religious renewal and revival as we enter the decline, as people look beyond themselves for answers, a conservative Republican leader with religious appeal could gain reelection. A conservative Republican administration without such a religious attraction will be sure to be thrown from office.

The Great Depression saw government taking the driver's seat in business, trying to steer the economy clear of the carnage created and left by the free markets of the 1920s.

Roosevelt and his New Deal were seen as the way out of the frustration and confusion of the early 30s. It is interesting to look back today, listening to the current talk of the evils of the Democratic party being so involved in the private sector during the New Deal, as if to say, "We have learned our lesson."

What form of government intervention will we see during the next downturn? Will we see a Republican president thrown from office in 1988 or 1992, remembered as the man in charge while the new era of pain was ushered in? These are interesting questions we will take a close look at later on.

The psychology of the long wave is affected enormously by the broad-base move towards conservative religious views as the decline deepens. We are told in scripture that Christ came to save the meek, the poor and the humble; all three categories have exploding populations during an economic downturn. The recent resurgence we have seen in fundamentalism is not due to the predictable long-wave re-alliance but is a reactionary response to the current advances in liberal social trends. However, these conservative movements will add strength to the new religious and social conservatism that emerges during the economic decline. When things are looking good and the economy is on the upswing, man looks within for his strength. We see positive thinking and get-rich quick seminars on the increase. We have witnessed this in the 70s and 80s. These are very similar to the flourishing self-help programs of the 20s. But as the tide turns and the chips are down the average man doesn't look within for strength but looks to secure institutions such as government, church and the union. I am not saying this is good or bad in and of itself but that it is a fact of the cycle.

The 1920s like the 70s and 80s had its own version of the sexual revolution. Stoken speaks of how women after just receiving the vote threw off the conventions of the Victorian period. Women began drinking and smoking in public and skirt lengths rose to the knee. Other changes were taking place: "There was a proliferation of sex magazines, which were gobbled up by a public obsessed with the subject. People liberated themselves from the restraints of puritanism. There was a vast increase in the divorce rate which rose from 8.8 for every 100 marriages in 1910 to 16.5 for every 100 marriages in 1928."

All these psychological changes took years to penetrate into the mainstream of society and emerge as the current social norms. Like a great wave moving through history, the long-wave cycle takes everything in its path.

Again, I must quote Stoken with his gifted perception into the psychology of the wave as he follows the social revolution into the downturn: "Initially, few people expect that a depression is going to last a long time. Most people think it is a cyclical contraction rather than a major change in the economy. The first sign that people no longer see the world in risk-free rose-colored terms often occurs with a subtle change in the relationship between the sexes. At the outset of the Great Depression, women lowered their skirts, dressed more conservatively, began to wear white gloves and became more respectful of a meal ticket. The sexual code was no longer flaunted so flagrantly. There was less ado about sex, while glamor and romance came into their own. The deepening depression shattered the assumptions of a relatively risk-free world that had dominated the mood of the 1920s. People became more cautious. Hedonistic behavior subsided and there was less tolerance of deviant social behavior.

"The younger generation became more respectful of their parents and less scornful of the old traditional values. The music slowed down. Marriage and the family became more highly prized as social institutions and the divorce rate fell. People stayed home and spent more time with their families."

Taking a holistic view of the long wave we see the enormous impact it has on politics, morality, religion and the family. It is a staggering thought that a cycle that has run its course only three times since the freedom of America could have an impact on a figure such as the divorce rate. It would seem that a force that has such an effect on society would be a valuable tool for decision making in our volatile world.

There is a vast amount of practical application for our knowledge of the effect on human nature of the rise and fall of the long wave. If indeed this wave exists with its seeming obvious impact on humanity, how can we use this information?

This chapter has emphasized the American model and how long-wave psychology affects it. Human nature is the same around the world and this chapter was not meant to limit its scope to America only. The reactions here apply to any peoples being pulled in one direction or the other by the long wave.

We cannot take too lightly the history of the wave and the potential force it has been shown to generate. This force could have an enormous impact on social and political change during the coming decline — an impact relevant to national safety and international stability. We can have at our disposal all the statistical data in the world, but if we cannot understand and perceive human nature and what man's response will be in situations beyond his immediate control, our data will be of no use.

A more sobering thought is the potential use of knowledge of the long wave for the execution of evil intentions. Knowledge of the long wave could be used to avert conflict or it could be used to assure that a conflict is settled in your favor, without consideration of what is right or wrong. In the wrong hands understanding of the long wave could be a powerful and evil tool.

Consider international strategic interest to the United States. The international political arena is volatile, to say the least, and the impact of the long wave on what direction and shape this volatility will take during a time of international economic decline is of immense concern to the United States as well as all other nations of the world. Being aware and ready for an economic decline and the instability it would bring could be the edge the United States would need to avert clashes that could lead to military escalation.

Consider the potential strains on East-West relations if Eastern Bloc countries are incapable of repaying their bills to their Western creditors during a commercial decline. As we will see later, an agricultural decline has been shown to be a major factor in the long wave; consider an international food shortage on top of an ailing international economic community. What will be the response of the human psychological factor under such conditions and how will it affect the balance of power or perhaps the emergence of a new centralized power based on economic considerations?

National and local elections are guided by the mood of the people and what they are looking for, thus a knowledge and understanding of the long wave could be of enormous importance to would-be candidates. The platform necessary for election or reelection during the most critical time of the cycle would be closely related to the psychological impact of the long wave on constituents. One could almost design a rough platform 10 years in advance by the known impact of an economic decline. We will take a closer look at the political considerations of the long wave at a later point.

So the long wave does not stand alone but measures and is guided by the psychological impulses of the world. It is a sobering thought that the long wave's psychological tendencies guide the destiny of nations.

After looking at the psychology of the long-wave cycle we gain a new respect for Jeremy Bentham and his view of man being guided by the two masters of pain and pleasure. There is no doubt that Western capitalist society has swung far in the direction of pleasure and if one were wise he would begin bracing for the inevitable pain as we swing back in the coming decline.

6

The Cycle and War

As long as man has kept records, he has been in conflict and at war with his fellow man. There are several periods during which the conflict has not been as widespread and destructive, but basically every period in man's history has seen war. However, an interesting pattern begins to emerge as we take a closer look. During the upswing of the long-wave cycle, there tends to be far more conflict than during the downswing.

As economies begin expanding and growing in individual nations of the world economy, nations tend to become competition for the other members of the system. Just as when an individual begins to establish himself economically and reach certain levels of success, he begins looking about to see what his next venture might be. Thus, as times are good, output is increasing, internally the economic outlook is stable and the domestic population is comfortable, national leaders begin to get restless and look beyond their borders to see where they may expand their influence.

The nation, just as the individual, will invariably step on someone's foot and that nation, just as the individual, will retaliate. It may be a dispute over scarce resources and raw materials or conflict over markets or just a restless leader seeking to expand his influence or use his military arsenal. Whatever the cause, conflict invariably tends to rise far more often during the upswing of the long wave than during the decline.

We will take a look only at the history of armed conflict since 1789 — the beginning of the upswing of the first long wave. A telling fact as we take an overview of war during this period is that the only time great powers were at war in modern times was during the upswing in the long-wave cycle. We must consider what a great power is in order to draw such a conclusion.

The book *War in the Modern Great Power System* by Jack

Levy was of great assistance to me in considering the relationship between the long-wave cycle and war.

The order of my review of war as well as the following quote is taken from that work:

"A Great Power is defined here as a state that plays a major role in international politics with respect to security-related issues. The Great Powers can be differentiated from other states by their military power, their interests, their behavior in general and interactions with other Powers, other Powers' perception of them and some formal criteria. Most important, a Great Power possesses a high level of military capabilities relative to other states. At a minimum, it has relative self-sufficiency with respect to military security. Great Powers are basically invulnerable to military threats by non-Powers and need only fear other Great Powers."

In looking at only 200 years of history we should perhaps refrain from drawing conclusions; but the evidence is impressive and we are tempted to look to the future and predict when the next major wars are likely to occur. Before trying our hand at predicting the future, let us take a close look at the past.

As stated earlier, the first of the long-wave cycles began its advance around 1789 and peaked in 1815. Our first major conflicts of this period were the French Revolutionary Wars from 1792 until 1802. The storming of the Bastille on July 14, 1789 marked the beginning of the revolution of France from a monarchy to a modern democratic nation. The coalition had its difficult moments as it went through its reconstruction period from 1789-91. The new constitution collapsed in 1792 and the new Legislative Assembly declared war on Austria on April 20, 1792, accusing them of counter-revolutionary agitation. This marked the beginning of 10 years of war fought from the Caribbean to the Indian Ocean, though most of the conflict was in the Low Countries, the Rhineland and Lombardy.

This period of the first upswing in long-wave theory is marked as the time western nations were finding their own and were beginning to lay the groundwork for the western capitalist nations that were to emerge. Those wars set the stage in France for the emergence of Napoleon. The French Revolutionary Wars saw the death of some 700,000 in battle while the Napoleonic Wars can be attributed close to 2 million deaths.

Napoleon Bonaparte proclaimed himself emperor in 1804 and waged war throughout Europe until 1815. These wars were really an extension of the French Revolutionary Wars in which the object of the allies of the nations of Europe was to stop French expansion. Napoleon was finally defeated by the Duke of Wellington at the Battle of Waterloo on June 18, 1815. The Napoleonic Wars were by far the most costly conflicts during the first upswing.

Other wars that deserve mention during this period are the Russo-Turkish War and the War of 1812. In the latter, America settled its independence from Britain once and for all, though not as quickly and decisively as we would have liked. The war lasted until January 1815 when Gen. Andrew Jackson won a decisive victory at New Orleans. A surging nationalism swept America after that victory where the British lost over 2,000 men and the Americans lost only 100.

The year 1815 saw the beginning of the decline of the first long wave. This decline continued until 1849. This 25-year period was virtually war-free, with the exception of the Franco-Spanish War which came about as France tried to interfere with the liberal revolution going on in Spain, April to August 1823.

Another conflict was the 1827 defeat of a Russian-British-French fleet at Navarino Bay by a Turkish-Egyptian fleet. This embarrassing defeat caused Russia to declare war in 1827 and came to be known as the Russo-Turkish War. During this conflict, "Russia invaded Bulgaria and forced Turkey to sign the treaty of Adrianople (1829), which recognized Greek independence, made Romania a Russian protectorate and gave Russia most of the Caucasian coast on the Black Sea," wrote Raymond.

The remainder of this first long-wave downturn seemed to scarcely produce a fist fight, so reserved were nations during this time of economic contraction.

As we enter the upswing of the second long-wave cycle and the economies of the nations of the world begin to expand, we again see an enormous increase in the number of wars and their devastation. The first incident of this period was the Austro-Sardinian War in 1849 which cost close to 6,000 lives. This same year saw the First Schleswig-Holstein War as well as the Roman Republic War; both were no more than brief skirmishes.

The next battle of this second upswing was the first major confrontation since Napoleon's defeat and is known as the Crimean War. Russia's desire to see the Ottoman Empire destroyed was the chief cause of the Crimean War and it would seem opportunity presented itself in 1852.

"The Crimean War has gone down in the history books as one of the worst managed, badly led, ill supplied and unnecessarily wasteful of life, of all modern wars," according to Bazancourt. "Battle after battle was marked by terrible blunders, on both sides. The famous charge of the Light Brigade was only one of these blunders, best known largely because it was immortalized in verse by Alfred, Lord Tennyson."

France, England, Prussia and Austria joined to fend off the aggression of Russia in the Crimean region. They were successful but at the expense of 500,000 lives. The Treaty of Paris on March 30, 1856, guaranteed independence to the Ottoman Empire. One of the good things which came out of the Crimean War was the work and leadership of Florence Nightingale, by whose work army hospitals and nurses came into existence.

The year 1856 also saw the Anglo-Persian War which lasted only four months and cost fewer than 1,000 lives. In 1859 the region that is now Italy began struggling for its economic independence. This led to the War of Italian Unification. All the major powers of Europe had to one degree or another interest in this area. But under the leadership of Garibaldi, the Italians fought for their freedom and established Rome as the capital of their new nation. The first national Italian Parliament met on February 18, 1861 and Victor Emmanuel II became king.

By far the bloodiest war of the upswing in the second long-wave cycle was the American Civil War, 1861-1865. The death toll by many estimates exceeded 500,000. Few will argue that the war was over anything more than conflicting economic interests of the North and the South during this time of rapid economic expansion. Not only was the slavery issue settled, but so was the issue of where the industrial strength of the United States would lie for years to come. The horror of the Civil War was that brother was pitted against brother, and father against son in a war that threatened to tear the young democracy apart.

Napoleon III was responsible for a number of French ventures during this period, one of which was the Franco-Mexican War, lasting from 1862 until 1867, in which some 8,000 died. The French army had put Maximilian on the Mexican throne but at the end of the Civil War the emperor was forced to remove his troops and the native Mexican forces were able to overthrow Maximilian.

The unification of Italy caused developments to the north that were settled by the Austro-Prussian War.

"With the appointment of Bismark as Prussian prime minister the struggle for German unification entered upon its last stage. It was settled by 'blood and iron' in the war of 1866," wrote Holborn. "Austria was supported by the southern German states in this struggle and fought successfully against the Italians on land and on the sea against Prussia's ally — Italy — but her main army was defeated at Sadowa on July 3, 1866 and the Prussian army could advance to the gates of Vienna. Austria ceded Venetia to Italy and resigned from German affairs."

The final major confrontation of this second upswing in the long wave came in the Franco-Prussian War, 1870-1871, in which 200,000 died. France lost and her government was left in shambles for attempting to avert the unification of Germany.

The second long wave began to peak and turn in 1873 and for almost 30 years the world economy slipped into a severe decline of previously unknown proportion. During this period the world was in a state of peace it had not known since the days of the Roman Empire. Two brief conflicts marked this period. One was the Russo-Turkish War, 1877-1878, which culminated with the treaty of Berlin (July 13, 1878). This war marks the greatest conflict in the past 200 years during a downswing of the long wave. This conflict saw 120,000 men lose their lives.

The other conflict during this time was the Sino-French War which took place from 1884-1885 and cost 2,100 lives. The year 1896 saw the bottom of the second decline and the beginning of the third advance of the long wave.

As would be expected, when nations began expanding their economies, war was not long in coming. The first war of this period came in 1904 — the Russo-Japanese War. Apparently Russia was exerting too much control and influence in Manchuria and Korea, causing the Japanese to get restless. Negotiations failed and Japan attacked the Russians in Port Arthur, Manchuria, on February 8, 1904, without a declaration of war. Japan had far superior organization and leadership as well as shorter supply lines and were able to deliver a final blow by destroying the Russian Baltic fleet at Tsushima (May 27-28, 1905). President Roosevelt arranged a peace conference at Portsmouth, New Hampshire, on August 5, 1905. Japan was granted her wishes in the region, but only after 45,000 men lost their lives.

The next conflict during this third upswing was the Italo-Turkish War (1911-1912). During this campaign the Italians were able to annex Libya at the price of some 6,000 lives. And of course the next war was "the war to end all wars," World War I (1914-1918). For the first time in history, the entire world — it seemed — was at war. The death and destruction were unimaginable. Close to 30 million lives were lost and the total cost of the war was over $180 billion. Did you ever stop to consider the real reasons for the war? It really stemmed from a conflict of economic interests between the nations involved. This war came during a surge in the industrialization of the world and nations were still securing colonies for the supply of raw materials and cheap labor.

The last confrontation of this third upswing came in the form of the Russian revolution. Nicholas II abdicated the throne on March 15, 1917, and for a brief time Russia was a democracy. But on October 24, 1917, the Bolsheviks, who were the most extreme of the revolutionaries, seized power. Thus we had the emergence of the Union of Soviet Socialist Republics. Surprisingly, there was not a great deal of bloodshed in the initial revolution; the bloodshed came in the form of internal purging later on.

The long wave peaked shortly after the close of the first world war and plateaued through the 20s and then fell dramatically in 1929 and the early 30s. This period, from the early 20s to the late 30s, was the third decline in the long-wave cycle. The world was once again fairly peaceful during this time of economic decline. The only wars to speak of during this time were the Manchurian War and the Italo-Ethiopian War in which a total of some 14,000 lives were lost.

From the beginning of World War II to the early 80s we were in the fourth advance of the long-wave cycle. Let us consider the wars which occured during this period.

The Sino-Japanese War began on July 7. 1937, over a minor clash of Chinese and Japanese soldiers on Marco Polo Bridge near Peking. This erupted into a bloody Far East war that was to merge four years later with World War II.

World War II has shown that one madman can have an impact on the long-wave cycle. This madman was none other than Adolf Hitler. His ruthless aggression once again brought the entire world into war. It is estimated that some 20 million lives were lost and the cost in property and monetary damages would be futile if not impossible to estimate. Hitler's quest for political and economic dominance over the world were chief reasons for the conflict as the world was once again struggling towards the upward swing of the long-wave cycle.

The Russo-Finnish War fought in 1939 and 1940 could be listed with World War II but was somewhat of a separate conflict and cost some 16,000 lives.

The communist revolution in China came to a close during

this period. While no one can be sure of the death toll, it was certainly in the millions.

The Korean War, 1950-1953, was the first military stance taken by the United Nations as it joined against communist aggression at a price of over 1 million lives to the participants.

The Russo-Hungarian War of 1956 cost some 7,000 lives and Hungarian hopes of more political and economic freedom.

The Vietnam War, 1962-1973, which cost 56,000 American lives, and the current Iran-Iraq War which started in 1979 are both wars which can be attributed to this fourth advance of the long wave.

In review of this chapter there emerges a startling fact that is overpowering and goes a long way to enforce the argument in favor of a long-wave cycle. This startling fact concerns the totals in the loss of life in the wars that have ravaged the world during the period from 1789 to the present. During long-wave downswings we have seen only several hundred thousand deaths from armed conflict while during long-wave upswings there have been in excess of 50 million deaths due to war.

The evidence speaks for itself. The world is far more likely to see war during the advance of the long wave than during the decline. This would lead us to the conclusion that if we are indeed in the plateau of the long wave and coming up on a decline, we should have a fairly peaceful world until early in the 21st century, at which time we can expect to see a rise in armed conflict among nations. This is not to say the world will be at total peace during this time but there should be no major conflict between Great Powers. There will always be small wars and eruptions on hostile borders during the long-wave decline.

I am in no way attempting to say that war guides the long-wave cycle, but just the opposite, as we see war as inevitable during the period of economic expansion that comes with the long-wave advance. It should be noted that since the long wave now has a tendency towards a lengthy advance and a short sharp decline, the next period of hostilities could come a bit sooner than would be normally anticipated.

All in all, war sheds a revealing light on the long wave and should be studied closely to understand and gain insight into the nature of this wave that has yet to fall from its fourth plateau and enter its fourth decline.

7

Bankers and Bad Times

Wall Street led the way in October of 1929 when the world experienced the market collapse due to the third decline of the economic long wave. The banks of the world were not long in following suit. In 1929 things were different than they are today. Wall Street has been regulated and curtailed in its speculative tendencies and no-money-down dice games.

But never fear, the bankers of today have taken up where Wall Street left off. Up to now we have been discussing the tide of history as the long wave has taken its course over the past 200 years. It is now time to get into the reality of the situation at hand and the predicament in which we now find ourselves.

The world banking system is in a condition it has not seen since the Great Depression and is perhaps far worse off than at that time. With some creative bookkeeping and a little help from Uncle Sam we have managed to keep it afloat. We heard quite a bit of talk in the early 80s about the impending doom of the financial world as we know it. Has the situation really changed? Is the banking system really on the way to recovery or is someone not telling us the whole story? Most of us are aware that Third World debt is being reshuffled faster than a deck of cards in a backroom poker game. After taking a close look at the situation I believe the safer money is in the poker game.

All types of debt are at unprecedented levels and this includes personal, corporate, Third World and not to mention the First World with the United States leading the way. We will first take a look at Third World debt which reached $1 trillion at the end of 1986. Our great banking institutions have loaned out over 100 percent of their equity to the Third World nations and by most estimates a majority of these loans are uncollectible. The developing nations are spending every available dollar to cover interest payments, a large part of which is being rolled over with the principal of these bad loans. It is absurd to believe the situation will eventually work its way out or that the poor nations of the world will eventually grow out of their debt. The loans will soon be rolled over one time too many and the world banking system will itself roll out of bed — and with it the world economy as we know it.

It doesn't take a Ph.D. in economics to realize that the game we are playing will one day have to come to an end.

Before discussing the day of reckoning, let's evaluate the situation in some hope of gaining an understanding of how we could have gotten ourselves into such a predicament.

Bankers came out of the Great Depression very conservative in nature as was everyone else. Interest rates were low and the industrial corporate world was expanding, providing safe havens for the banker's abundance of free cash. And free cash it was, as the humble public would never ask for such a thing as to earn interest-on-demand deposits. So the bankers found themselves in a position that was hard to beat.

As the upswing got under way, however, the public became a demanding group and began putting money in places that appreciated the value of a dollar and were willing to pay the customer for his considerate deposit. The bankers figured they were doing the public a favor by opening their doors from 10 a.m. till 2 p.m. and were under an illusion of their worth and service to humanity. Banks were slow in understanding the gravity of the shift in consumer demand. The thrifts and savings and loans had cut deeply into the banks' bottom line before bankers began seeking solutions to the growing problem. This new-found competition, coupled with rising interest rates and inflation on an upward trend, as it always is in the upswing of the long wave, forced bankers to evaluate closely their situation and use a bit more creativity in their dealings.

A number of the big banks struck on the idea of making high-yielding loans to the developing Third World. Bankers have an acute tendency towards the herding instinct, so when the giants such as Chase, Citicorp and Chemical began loaning to the Third World the entire world banking community figured it was a good thing to do.

A nation is sovereign and lives a perpetual existence, not like the corporation which can turn bottom up and vanish when times get bad. This seemed to play a major role in the thinking of the world bankers during the late 60s and 70s as they could somehow not perceive a nation or state becoming insolvent. As we will soon see, "sovereignty is not a substitute for solvency," as a wise man once said.

With a bunch of western bankers in pin-striped suits waving billions of dollars in their faces, the leaders of the Third World were more than happy to oblige the bankers and take the money off their hands. This is not to say that the leaders of the Third World were forced to take the loans and are thus not responsible for the current crisis situation. They are very much responsible and should be held so.

They were well aware of the amount of debt they were taking on and what the limits were of the countries they ruled. What they were not aware of was the shifting tide of the world economy and the havoc played by runaway inflation and depressed economic conditions on a nation that must sell its goods on the world market to pay its massive loans. These nations cannot default because they have needs other than paying their interest. The world banking community is the only place they can find these funds. If they default they would never again be able to acquire credit on the world markets. It is as well in the best interest of the banks for the countries not to default; a somewhat obvious conclusion as the banks would become insolvent and the world economy would fall like dominos.

The fact of the matter is that the billions of dollars lent to the Third World are uncollectible and should be written off the books of our banks.

Julian M. Snyder, editor and publisher of *International Moneyline* and a longtime proponent of the long wave, gives a sobering account of the condition of these loans: "According to our studies, directed by a former bank officer, conservative discounting of the loans would put three of our major banks — Citicorp, Chase and Manufacturer's Hanover — into a negative net-worth position. If all foreign loans were discounted by 50 percent, we would have to add Chemical Bank and Banker's Trust to the top nine United States banks we looked at. In my view, a 75-percent discount would be more realistic. On such a basis, all nine banks would have a negative net worth and, from a technical accounting viewpoint, would be insolvent. These banks, incidentally, have 60 percent of the foreign loans to Mexico and also about 60 percent of the loans to Brazil.

"Obviously, while we can raise questions about solvency, these banks are liquid because they are still functioning. You can still write a check to pay your dentist or telephone bill. But from a strictly accounting viewpoint, the proliferating propo-

sals for write-offs and stretch-outs implicitly adopt the view
that the problem is insolvency — not illiquidity."

The bad times facing the bankers are not coming just from
the Third World. Such has our attention because of the enormous
amount of money owed. As one looks at the corporate situation
in America today, another element to the impending banking
doom begins to show its face. Corporations are currently in
debt-to-equity situations and debt-to-working-capital and debt-
to-available cash positions as have not been seen since the Great
Depression. Banks are failing at record rates in agricultural and
energy regions in the United States, clearly due to the overproduction in agriculture and energy industries that is causing prices
to fall.

States such as Texas and others are changing their laws to
make it easier for outside banks to take over their troubled banks
in an effort to avert a panic. This is only a surface solution and
doesn't address the underlying problems.

Many banks are finding themselves in a great deal of trouble because of overproduction in commercial properties. Prices
are falling and borrowers are finding themselves unable to repay
their loans. What we see is only a sign of what is to come in the
rest of the economy. How long can the current situation last?
Soon the game will be over and the financial house of cards
created during the upswing will come tumbling down.

Even without the Third World debt, sooner or later corporate expansion will begin to slow. We will also see a slow-
down in the spending of the individual. There invariably comes a
time when the corporation, the government and the individual
has borrowed beyond his limit. This has always happened in the
peak of the long-wave cycle, causing spending — thus expansion
— to come to a screeching halt.

An important point the public should be aware of is that
the FSLIC and FDIC insurance agencies for banking institutions
are really not supported by law. That is to say that if enough
banks go under in the coming collapse, the federal government
has no responsibility by law to refund depositors' money if the
insurance agencies run dry of funds. A recent report by the General Accounting Office stated the FSLIC is operating with a $6
billion deficit. That's not what I consider a reliable insurance
company. The belief that these agencies could survive a major
downturn is only wishful thinking.

James Grant, who is a former *Barron's* bond reporter and is
now editor of *Grant's Interest Rate Observer*, gives us these

"encouraging" words in relation to a banking failure: "Anyone who assumes that 'they' are not going to let this happen is making a profound miscalculation. The FDIC, FSLIC and Farm Credit Bank are all broke or nearly broke. And so much credit has been created outside the banking system that the Federal Reserve Board now regulates a less and less significant sector."

Robert Prechter, the well-known and respected editor of the *Elliot Wave Theorist,* has some fascinating insights into the banking problems: "The idea that government can insure the banks has made them more unsafe, not less, because it has encouraged them to take imprudent risks. Many are technically bankrupt right now. During the crash, so many bank loans will go sour that the government will have to declare a national bank moratorium. They won't call it a default. They'll say, 'You still have your money but you can't touch it until next year.' Of course, that year will stretch into many. The ensuing depression could last until the year 2000. Ultimately, the only thing you'll want to own is bullion-style gold coins. Gold will be the only sure store of value."

There are those who believe the power invested in the Federal Reserve Board by the Monetary Control Act of 1980 will eliminate destructive deflationary pressures. This is an understandable mistake, but I must disagree. The Fed was given power to buy foreign bonds and loans and reduce the reserve requirements of our banks to zero. The theory that creating money in this manner will stop disinflation (slowing increases in prices) and deflation (falling prices), has proven not to hold water.

Over the past five years we have seen a great deal of loosening of the money supply with rising figures of M1 and M2 (figures for the amount of money in the economy), yet we have had disinflation and deflation of prices during this same period. In 1986 M1 or the basic money supply increased by 17 percent which matches the level reached during the peak of inflation in the late 70s. The difference is that this time around inflation on the retail level rose by only 1.1 percent in 1986.

Today there is so much slack in the economy with industry operating at less than 80 percent capacity that large increases in the money supply still don't inflate prices. Industry scrambles to fill increases in demand and is forced to keep prices low to attract any new business. Prices are incapable of moving up any sustainable extent when the economy is operating at far below capacity.

What is clearly happening to the money created by the Fed

is that it is pouring into the stock markets where it is encouraging and fueling financial inflation or bull markets throughout the world. The Fed is creating paper millionaires, not inflation. The Fed is at a loss to understand why their loose money policies have not ignited inflation to any substantial degree. The fact is that the only way one can come to a clear understanding of the situation we are facing is by taking the all-encompassing view as seen by long-wave theory.

Deflationary pressures are at this time building as the long wave takes its course and no monetary manipulation will be able to stop the inevitable. As the amount of world debt in all sectors continues to mount and the sliding real values of commodities, capital outlays and capital expansion become evident, the buying power of the world will be eroded even further.

Where are the nations, corporations and individuals who can afford to take on the money that the Fed intends to create? The idea that the Monetary Act of 1980 can stop deflation is simply invalid. When the Fed realizes that the money it creates is only fueling the raging bull markets of the world they will slam on the breaks and by so doing will push the world economy over the edge. The Fed will prove to be impotent in trying to avoid the inevitable flow of the long-wave cycle.

The lack of buying power in the world economy will cause world prices to continue to slide as the decline begins. Many will be under the illusion that as prices begin to slow and fall that this will bring in more buying strength. Prices may pick up a bit in the late 80s as the plateau takes its full illusionary effect. Buying strength, thus prices, may pick up for a short season but it will not last. The nations, the companies and the individuals will eventually simply not be able to afford any more spending on borrowed money. Because of the continued and increasing weakness in demand across the board, prices will tumble. The slowdown will force layoffs and firings, thus eroding buying strength and demand even further. As the long wave declines after this plateau we are seeing here in the mid-80s, the prices of raw materials, wholesale goods, commodities, as well as consumer goods and real estate will collapse. We have seen radical drops in raw materials and commodities prices since 1981. The forces generating these drops will soon be seen throughout all industries and the entire economy. The effect of falling prices will snowball into the crash and once again the Indian summer boom of the long-wave plateau will have ended. First it will be disinflation but as we enter the decline we will see deflation across the board. Deflation means only one thing for the banking community — trouble. This natural turning in the long wave will be fueled by an important element in our new world economy and the chief means by which a majority of the Third World debt is being repaid.

This important element and wild card is the price of oil. Mexico, Argentina, Indonesia and Nigeria pay on loans with oil export revenues. If prices fall low enough, oil-exporting Third World nations will not even be able to pay interest. The burden will be so great they will be forced to default. Package after package will be put together by the IMF and World Bank, but eventually the game will be over and the world banking system will suddenly give in and admit its insolvency.

We saw oil prices peak in 1980 and have seen them gradually sliding ever since with extensive drops in the past year. OPEC seems to be at the point of breaking up at this time as Saudi Arabia is slashing its prices in an attempt to recover its lost market share. The nations with heavy debt are being forced to increase production as prices drop, thus forcing more downward pressure as well as increasing the threat of other OPEC members to glut the market.

By some estimates if oil drops below $12 a barrel for any extended period of time, Mexico and others would be forced to default, by no choice of their own. The amounts of default will be so great that no juggling act by the IMF, World Bank or Washington will help the situation. It is conceivable that if the world was in a period of expansion and growth at the same time of this default that a package could be put together to save the world banking system from collapse.

This simply will not be the case in the late 80s, as we have discussed earlier; the corporation, nation and the individual will be slamming on the breaks and the world economy will slide over the edge into the next decline of the long-wave cycle.

Before continuing, I would like to introduce some very sobering thoughts on the effects of oil prices on the coming crash of the western world's financial system. These thoughts, which outline a very real threat in today's changing world, should send shudders up the spines of strategy planners from oil company boardrooms to the Pentagon's war room.

The Soviet Union has for some time now been the largest oil producer in the world and the potential oil fields of that vast nation are so enormous as to make Exxon green with envy.

By the late 80s the Soviets could well be exporting over

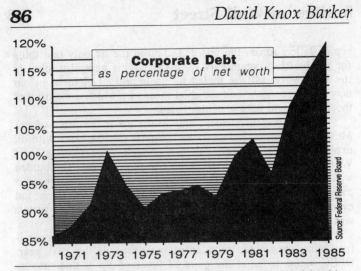

Corporate Debt
as percentage of net worth

Source: Federal Reserve Board

4 million barrels of oil a day and hold the international banking community in the palm of its hand with the threat to slash oil prices to even lower levels than they will be at that time. Such an action would soon cause the world bankers' house of cards to come crashing down.

Perhaps that is a far-fetched idea, but in a volatile world we must come to expect the unexpected. Many are under the illusion that the Soviets would never do such a thing because they must purchase grain with oil revenues to feed their people. We mustn't forget with whom we are dealing; many Russian peasants in past decades thought the government would never do particular things perceived clearly as against its own interest. We are not dealing with a benign, loving dictatorship nor a Marxian utopia that figures first in its equations the element of human suffering. We are dealing with a belief system that would like to enslave the world with its perverted economic religion.

Action in Soviet oil markets will be one of the more interesting developments as the price of oil on world markets continues to weaken. The Soviet natural gas pipeline to Europe could also be used to undermine prices, thus may yet prove an instrument of Soviet action and intentions. The Soviets have a great deal to gain from the monetary system that will emerge from the coming financial carnage and would not in the least be disturbed with a mere collapse of the West's monetary system.

Occurences in the Persian Gulf region will play an important role in oil prices as well as the whole international economy. If full-scale war erupts, oil prices will certainly be pushed up. I be-

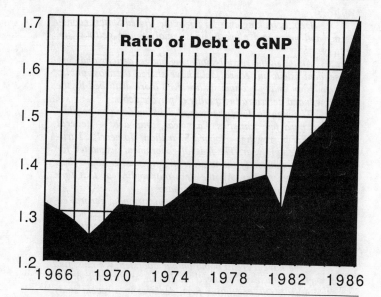

Ratio of Debt to GNP

lieve the support level is more in the neighborhood of $10 a barrel before the Third World defaults across the board. I believe we will see oil prices fluctuate from the $15- to the $20-level throughout the next few years. But the natural forces of supply and demand will eventually drive oil prices down sharply.

Even an oil import tax imposed by Washington will only prop prices up for a limited length of time before oversupply pushes them down again. Though oil prices are a crucial factor, they don't hold the only key to the coming collapse. As the entire world economy slows, other forces will eventually and of necessity force all prices down. Oil prices cannot be given total credit for the coming banking collapse and economic decline but should be looked upon as a major force that will lead the economy into deflation.

As we have discussed, oil is only one of many troubled sectors in the economy which is forcing banks to close their doors. Virtually every sector of the economy will be placing pressure on the banking system. The straw that finally breaks the camel's back could come from any number of places.

Alfred L. Malabre Jr. and Lindley H. Clark Jr. in a February 2, 1987 article in *The Wall Street Journal* outline clearly the pressure debt is placing on the economy and on the survival of the banks:

> *Debt is bulking ever larger in the United States econo-*
> *my and more and more business analysts are getting jit-*
> *tery...*
> *Although the record-shattering budget deficits and con-*
> *sequent pileup in federal debt have stirred the most public*
> *discussion, many economists are even more disturbed by the*
> *growth and deteriorating quality of private debt...*
> *The magnitude of the overall debt buildup can be illus-*
> *trated by a few statistics. Last year, total debt — federal*
> *plus other borrowing — topped $7 trillion. Up nearly $1 tril-*
> *lion in a single year. The federal government accounted for*
> *about one-quarter of the total, a slightly smaller share than*
> *two decades earlier. All the debt outstanding at that time*
> *was about equal to last year's increase.*
> *The surge in debt, moreover, is outstripping general ec-*
> *onomic growth. Debt now totals about 1.7 times gross nation-*
> *al product. That's the highest such ratio since the worst years*
> *of the Depression, when the nation's output of goods and*
> *services shrank and bankruptcies soared ...*
> *"We have a credit bomb on our doorstep. We must find*
> *a way to defuse it," Lowell L. Bryan, a director of the*
> *McKinsey & Co. consulting firm, declares in a recent study*
> *for the Harvard Business School....*
> *Even without a recession this year, L. William Seid-*
> *man, the FDIC chairman, expects more than 150 banks to*
> *fail. Besides the mounting failures, he adds, "there are about*
> *1,500 problem banks on our list."*

A major banking collapse has come with the decline of every long wave since 1789 and each collapse has been followed by
major changes in the financial system of the world. The Great
Depression and the banking collapse of 1933 saw the world come
off the gold standard and we saw fiat money (money not backed
up by a commodity) enter as the new standard for international
transactions. This collapse also prompted more power to be
granted to the Federal Reserve and an overall centralization of
banking in the United States and the world.

Circumstances created by a major banking collapse could
force creative and necessary innovations to strengthen and stabi-
lize our world economy. These changes could make the entire
world more productive and generate a rising standard of living
for the entire world community.

Innovations that are needed but painful often must be
spurred on by unavoidable catastrophe. Only when the economy
is in a state of disarray and confusion are the changes made.

What changes will come with the coming collapse of the

international monetary system during this high-tech age of the computer and microprocessor? What effect will our shrinking world community and economy have on the new system that will emerge from the financial carnage created by the coming collapse?

The only reason catastrophe has been avoided in the past few years in the international banking arena has been the revival of the U.S. economy. This is just as we saw in the past plateau of the long wave from 1922 to 1929, before the last great downturn in the long wave.

With this revival and pickup in world trade beginning late in 1982, the IMF (International Monetary Fund) and the World Bank were able to scrape together enough funds from public and private sources to loan the Third World enough money to pay the interest on their existing loans.

What is going to happen when we once again slide into a slight recession? What brought the world economy crashing in 1929 was that the three-and-one-half year cycle, the seven- to 11-year cycle and the long wave all met turning down at one time in 1929, which resulted in the Great Depression.

Kondratieff believed the intermediate cycles acquire a stamp from the long wave. The slight drawback we saw in 1986 for all practical purposes was unnoticeable as the strong push forward during the last few years of the plateau of the long wave gave momentum to the economy. The underlying forces and changes occurring distort the intermediate and short cycle. Like a dying animal that thrashes in the last few moments of its life, the world economy will struggle and give one last heroic effort before entering into the long-wave decline.

Once again the meeting in unison of the three waves of economics: the three-and-one-half-year cycle, the seven- to 11- year cycle and the long-wave cycle will be devastating. The only difference in 1929 and the coming collapse is that in 1929 the stock market was leading the way. This time around there is the great possibility that the stock market will be following on the heels of the international banking system.

8

Trade Wars

It may be obvious that during a long-wave economic decline there would also be a decline in the volume of world trade. This has proven to be the case in all three long-wave declines of the past 200 years yet deserves close attention so that we may gain an understanding of the nature of this trade decline as well as its place and role in the long wave.

The growing trend towards protectionism and trade barriers we have witnessed over the past few years is not a unique phenomenon of today. The late 20s were experiencing the same pressure, as was the case during the early 70s of the 19th century, not to mention the conditions in the years just before the defeat of Napoleon in 1815 in Europe as the old country was being swamped by goods from America.

As the world comes out of a long-wave decline, interest rates are low and the world has been flushed of its excess debt. New inventions and products are beginning to take hold and business begins to pick up as the world comes out of its cautious withdrawn state of decline. Labor is cheap and people are willing to work hard as they have learned to appreciate holding a job after a period of severe unemployment. Workers are willing to sacrifice to get the economy rolling after experiencing the pain of the hard times during the decline. Markets are beginning to open up as trade picks up all over the world in anticipation of better days to come.

The world is still cautious during this time and companies are extremely risk-averse and will not take the chance of expanding beyond what they know for sure the markets will sustain. The work-ethic gains renewed validity during this time as the world is slowly moving into a state of recovery and renewed optimism about the future and what it holds. World prices begin to come out of their slump as the demand for products is on the rise. When the upswing is just getting under way there is a

91

push for open trade and the elimination of barriers. Companies are eager to peddle their wares on foreign soil and to give others the right to do the same since the marketplace is once again demanding products.

Producers have been streamlined and made more efficient during the decline and are willing to support the tearing down of the tariffs and barriers prohibiting international trade. Interest rates and wages are low so as prices begin to pick up profits are beginning to soar. With high profits and booming business there is enormous force in the international marketplace to open borders and have much freer trade laws.

Soon the world economy is in full swing and the international marketplace is once again making its way up the long wave of economic expansion. As the years roll on, there is a turnover in leadership in the world economy and the new blood does not remember the last major decline. This has the effect of draining most of the pessimism and caution out of the system. Corporations, individuals and the sovereign state become willing to pay more for the right to borrow money as the advance strengthens. Companies are willing to take on more and more debt to keep up with the competition and expand their market share.

As interest rates climb during the upswing of the long wave, it becomes harder and harder for companies to cover their expenses. Without understanding the long-wave forces at work, this would seem odd during this time of increased trade and productivity. Sales are increasing and business is booming but as we move further into the advance it is becoming more and more difficult to meet the bottom line as profit margins are beginning to shrink; this changes as we enter the plateau as we will see later.

Labor-intensive industries are beginning to flow towards less developed nations with cheaper labor and less restrictions on the use of that labor. During the upswing, when times are good, there is a tendency towards overcapitalization and investment in layouts even though the price that is paid on the money that is used for these layouts in the form of interest is getting more expensive.

Because of the overexpansion there is increased competition for the existing market as well as a tendency towards overproduction as the new capacity comes on line, thus flooding the market and forcing prices down.

A classical example of this is the world oil industry. The oil industry geared up for the expansion of the 50s, 60s and 70s and production capacity far exceeded the world's need for oil. A great deal of money was borrowed from Western banks and used to upgrade and expand refinery and production facilities in the Third World. Those facilities are now aiding in the overproduction of oil, thus forcing prices down and making the Third World incapable of paying its loans. We have seen this happen in numerous markets from textiles to microchips as there has been an overcapitalization in virtually every industry during the upswing of the long-wave cycle.

This overexpansion during a time of higher interest rates begins to show up in the way of shrinking profit margins. As we get further and further into the upswing it becomes more difficult to make a dollar in the marketplace.

One of the most important aspects of the shrinking profit picture and the more competitive marketplace is the effect on trade among nations. Pressure begins to build for more protection from government, as in recent years the introduction of legislation for barriers and tariffs is on the rise. This has not been confined to Washington. Every capital in the world has begun to feel the pressure. Of course trade barriers are treating the symptom and not the cause and will make the problem far worse. Although the long wave would take its course with or without the element of trade barriers emerging in the top of the upswing, I believe we should take a brief look at the emergence of this new attitude which we will consider to be the "ignorance of protectionism."

In a speech delivered November 6, 1986 to the Americas Society in New York City, David Peterson, the Premier of Ontario, presented some startling thoughts on the current tides of international trade. Here are a few highlights:

> *We are all aware of the consequences incurred when the international trading system collapsed after the adoption of such measures as the Smoot-Hawley Tariff of 1930 and the British Tariff of 1932.*
>
> *The sudden surge of protectionism snapped a golden age of trade, cutting down assembly lines and creating soup-lines, closing banks and foreclosing farms.*
>
> *The foundations of those protectionist trade walls bear a remarkable resemblance to trends we see today, more than a half-century later.*
>
> *The trade wars of the 20s and 30s were sparked by slow growth in demand for traditional goods and services; a sudden spread of technological knowledge which narrowed competitive gaps between nations; an abrupt decline in the*

*need for raw materials; and rapid shifts in the balance of
market power.*

*The similarities to today's conditions remind me of the
words of a great philosopher, Yogi Berra: "It's deja vu all
over again."*

Making intelligent decisions and not being carried on the
protectionist emotion of the day in relation to international
trade would not stop the eventual downturn of the long wave
but it would certainly eliminate a great deal of unnecessary pain
and hardship on the world. There are currently hundreds of proposals before Congress for the protection of American industry
from foreign competition. These proposals threaten to help force
the world over the edge and into the next decline and make it
more harsh and lengthy than it has to be.

I do not support the sacrifice of domestic business for international development. This is not even the case as many assume it to be. There does not have to be a decrease in the Western world's standard of living in order to have an increase in the
rest of the world. This notion is no more than a bold face lie.
Under an effectively managed economy the whole world could
realize an increase in living standards. Companies fighting for
protectionism believe the people of the world should be forced
to subsidize and pay the bill for their inefficiencies and lack of
responsibility in taking on more debt than they could handle and
expanding beyond the needs of the world economy. These companies are not willing to face the irresistible trends toward a
world economy and admit the foolish mistakes they made.

The fact is that the domestic economies within the world
economy are hurt by protectionism and not helped; but, more
importantly, the brunt of this inefficiency falls on the consumer. The lifeblood of the economy is the discretionary income of
the consumer and is the economic factor most threatened by protectionist policy. The storm clouds of trade war are forming on
the horizon as they have in the past when we have moved into
the peak of the long wave and, if allowed to continue, the coming decline will be far deeper and darker than necessary. It is accepted by most that the Great Depression was far deeper and
lengthier than it should have been due to the growing international trade isolationism.

What makes a democratic political system strong is that
the individual is the central element; personal freedom and dig-
nity are what make the system work. Likewise, what makes the
world's free-market system work is that the consumer is grant-

ed freedom to choose and to have free access in his decision making; the consumer is to be the central force and pivotal element of the free-market system. The consumer free of constraints creates the economic phenomenon of demand and the business sector free of restraints or props responds in the economic phenomenon of supply. Protectionism injected into the system is a poison which distorts both supply and demand and creates inefficiency and waste in the system.

There are enormous hidden costs in protectionism which stifle the economy. The Center for the Study of American Business at Washington University released a study in 1983 which should deter the protectionist warlords but has not proven to enlighten their self-centered ignorance. Adjusting for inflation, the American consumer in 1982 paid foreign governments and foreign manufacturers conservatively more than $4 billion for textile and apparel quotas alone. Tack on another $19 billion for the tariffs, which are a tax we pay our government on the value of apparel entering this country. That comes to $23 billion dollars we paid for textiles and apparels alone which could have gone to revitalizing and spurring growth in our economy.

Can we in any way rationalize these enormous costs? Some poor fool will invariably ask, "how many jobs did these restraints save?" The cost per job saved is indefensible. Several studies have been done which show a cost-benefit ratio of trade restrictions: Consumers, you and I, pay an estimated $110,000 a year in higher prices to save a $24,000-a-year job in steel, $77,000 a year to save a $8,000-a-year job in footwear and $80,000 a year for a $10,000-year job in textiles. Don't think I'm going to leave the displaced worker at the unemployment office. Eliminate the barriers and for each displaced textile and apparel worker you've got savings that could go to transaction assistance. Of course only a fraction of the savings would go into retraining assistance. The rest would go into the pockets of the consumers and back into the economy for growth.

In remembering that for every action there is an equal and opposite reaction, we must consider what protectionism in Washington will bring in retaliation from Tokyo, Seoul, London, Peking and Taipei. In looking at the past, it would appear the reaction is often stronger than the action. For example, in 1983 we restricted $55 million worth of cotton blouses from China; China retaliated by cancelling $500 million worth of orders for American grain, a brilliant move by our farsighted Congress. This is an excellent example of how protection of one industry shifts the burden onto another. As one nation blocks trade, the nation that is hurt will surely retaliate and the entire world will suffer. These situations only emphasize the reality of an international economy that is here to stay and protectionist hypocrisy that has got to go.

Competition and the free market are what make the American and world economy work. We need to do all we can to support the removal of constraints and allow the consumer to make his choice unrestrained by the inconsistencies and greed of the protectionists. It is perhaps too late for substantial action to be taken to ensure free trade, as we are already on the plateau of the long wave and the push for protection is overpowering.

In 1947 the General Agreement on Tariffs and Trade (GATT) was signed by the United States and a majority of the nations of the world and even though this agreement and subsequent agreements have done a great deal to insure free trade they are not enough to restrain the protectionist tendencies that are building. The decline always brings great changes to the forefront in international trade and there is no doubt that we will see even more powerful treaties and agreements to bring us out of the coming decline to insure an even freer world economy in the next upswing.

John Oliver Wilson, chief economist at Bank of America, has observed the potential of a repeat in history in the area of protectionism: "This is not the first time in our history that the threat of trade wars has erupted. And it is useful to briefly recall this history, for the lessons from the past can serve us well in the present. In 1930, the United States passed the Smoot-Hawley Act which broadened tariff coverage to 25,000 products and provided for substantial increases in over 800 tariff rates. The reaction of the rest of the world was immediate. Widespread protests erupted. Tariffs were raised in a dozen major countries and they were targeted against American products. The League of Nations, which was working hard to halt the upward trend in tariffs, was powerless. The seeds of economic isolation had been deeply planted."

It would seem that the trend towards protectionism in this fourth peak of the long-wave cycle is too far out of control to be stopped before great damage is done. Most leaders are aware of the harm done by protection but are powerless to stop the spreading disease, especially in the U.S., where lawmakers are so quick to cater to the needs of their constituents in the hope of reelection. This sort of blind, foolish action must be stopped and it would seem that the only way to do so is to take the authority out of the hands of the lawmakers who are so susceptible to bribery and turn it over to an international body for even stronger action to insure a free-market system.

As we peak in the late 80s there will no doubt be uncontrollable pressure for protection on all fronts.

Wilson is again very perceptive as he probes the reasons for this self-defeating protectionism: "Isolated in their economic policies, unwilling to compromise on their economic and political principles, strong-willed in their personal individualism, the outcome is hardly surprising: The leaders of the free world are rapidly moving down the road of protectionism and economic autarky."

It is a fact of life that catastrophe often breeds innovation and this includes science, politics and economics. As the world plunges into the next decline and barriers are thrown up everywhere to protect ailing industries who have expanded beyond world demand with expensive capital, the situation will get so bad as to force coordination of action towards solving the problem. Perhaps we shouldn't dread too much the coming decline because it will invariably produce sweeping changes in our world economy and most surely it will produce a radical change in policy among trading partners of the world. These changes will guarantee free trade and open borders not seen since the days of the Roman Empire.

The world over we are finding a new acceptance of impending change in the world trading arena and a sense of the acceptance of eventually finding a better way to do things. The coming decline may well give the leaders of the world the reason to go ahead and make the changes that are so necessary.

As we continue to look at the long wave, it becomes obvious that it takes everything in its path as it moves through history.

In this chapter we have seen that world trade is no exception. There is no doubt that the economic conditions and forces that brought about the protectionism of the last three peaks in the long-wave cycle exist today.

In conclusion, we must acknowledge that before the current tension subsides, the world once again faces a major trade decline.

9

The Failing Farm

Falling land prices, high interest rates, sliding commodity prices and enormous amounts of debt sound like a few of the problems that are facing the farmers of the 1980s, as is the case, but this is also the situation farmers were facing in the mid-1920s. Is this repeat of the farming crisis just a coincidence, a fluke that has no real significance, or does the long wave also include a decline in agriculture as a result of the forces at work as the world economy peaks and prepares for the next decline?

American and European agriculture was suffering fearfully around the time of the defeat of Napoleon in 1815. This was the case again in the late 1860s just prior to the second downturn of the long wave. Are these agricultural declines — all gathered around the peak of the long waves — isolated incidents unrelated as to their causes and timing? Long-wave theory suggests not.

As Kondratieff emphasized so effectively, prices peak and begin to drop in long-wave theory due to overexpansion which brings overproduction. This erosion of prices does not happen automatically, across the board, but begins slowly, first in land prices and raw materials and then works its way up until it finally reaches consumer goods and luxury items. The farmer is caught in a squeeze because he is paying high prices which are still rising for machinery and production products while the price he is getting for his produced goods is falling. Caught in the middle during a period of rising interest rates and falling demand on world markets for his products, the farmer is the first to feel the pain of the coming decline.

One would ask at this point why it is prices first begin to fall on farmland and in agricultural and commodity products? The answer lies in factors that are explained in detail in Chapter 10 on technology and invention and are centered on high-priced technology that is developed during the decline and implemented during the upswing. This new technology helps to pull agriculture out of its slump and makes it more productive through new chemicals and machinery. Through new innovation and processes the farm becomes far more efficient and competitive on the world market. The improved technology and productivity pushes agriculture into a period of overproduction as the long wave enters its last leg of the advance.

We are all aware that food is the most basic of human needs that will be met before man delves into other projects as the upswing is getting under way. There is a change in priorities during a decline. Things which seemed to be important as man moved into the peak of the long wave, such as sports cars and mink coats, are given a back seat to agriculture. But sure as the world economy peaks again, agriculture, as it enters its phase of overproduction, takes a back seat to the luxuries of life.

Food is a priority which will be met before man endeavors to meet his other less basic needs. Herein lies the reasons for agriculture being the first to begin the upswing of the long-wave cycle and why it is the first area to implement the new technology developed during the decline. It could also be said that agricultural products being the most basic and practical of all products give a better reflection of true value, so they dictate to the rest of the market what prices should be doing and are thus a leader as the economy goes into a deflationary period. This is to say that agriculture clearly makes the statement that enough is enough and it is time for world prices to come back to earth.

In discussing the trade decline in the last chapter we clearly presented that as we enter a period of overproduction in the world economy this forces us to a peak in the cycle. Because agriculture was the first area to gear up and pull out of the decline, it is only natural that it should be the first to enter a period of overcapitalization and overproduction as we are seeing today. This explains why in the past three long-wave cycles there was a decline in agriculture first, followed by a decline in the rest of the economy. This should cause us to take a bit more sobering look at the current predicament of agriculture all over the world.

The agricultural decline is in no way independent of the rest of the long-wave cycle but is an integral part of the entire cycle. Being out of rhythm with the rest of the cycle costs the agricultural economy dearly. As we reach the top of the cycle we see agriculture put in a triple squeeze. Agriculture is first caught in the situation of rising operating cost and falling land and commodity prices. These price shifts come during a period of high interest rates. To top it off agriculture is asked to do business in a world of growing international protectionism. This is especially difficult since agriculture is the United States' largest export. The pressure is just too much and the farming community is thrown into depression 10 years earlier than the rest of the world economy. Visit any midwest farming town and you will see that no one in these areas is under the illusion of an expanding growing economy as people are in the rest of the world. The farming community is but a reflection of what the rest of the world will soon be experiencing.

A December 24, 1986, article in *The Wall Street Journal* gives exceptional insight into the situation on the farm today and clearly presents the long-wave elements which are present...

> *The farm economy, still burdened by tremendous overcapacity, is merely pausing before another long bleed, many economists say ...*
>
> *The Farm Belt faces at least three or four more years of radical shrinkage, many economists say. Capital will be slowly wrung out of the sector, as lenders eventually push billions of dollars of land onto the market at lower and lower prices. As the farm depression drags on, a swelling number of farmers and farm suppliers will lose the war of attrition and some analysts see the exodus of the next four years exceeding that of the last four ...*
>
> *Certainly, for some farmers and suppliers, the worst is over. Land prices, having plunged more than 50 percent in some areas, won't fall as far or as fast in the future ...*
>
> *Excess capacity will plague U.S. agriculture for the next decade, a study by the Food and Agriculture Policy Research Institute suggests. It predicts that enough land will come out of production as the result of federal policy or economic pressures to restore equilibrium by the mid-1990s. But idled land is still there and if farmers again planted all available acres, they would still produce about 30 percent too much wheat and 35 percent too much cotton, the study calculates ...*
>
> *Meanwhile, overhanging the farm-land market is a huge portfolio of land in the hands of agriculture lenders. They have acquired millions of acres that collateralized bad debt. Many would love to be rid of it but, reluctant to recognize big losses or to depress the market, have held off selling land in the hope prices will rise.*
>
> *But the backlog itself is more than enough to torpedo any general recovery in land prices. As of Septem-*

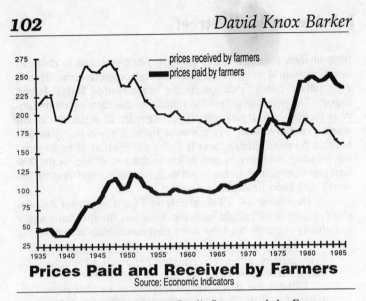

Prices Paid and Received by Farmers
Source: Economic Indicators

ber 30, the federal Farm Credit System and the Farmers Home Administration, two of the largest farm lenders, held a combined total of 3.4 million acres of agricultural land — a chunk larger than the state of Connecticut. The holdings are valued at nearly $2 billion. Commercial banks and insurance companies are believed to own at least an additional $1 billion worth ...

Mr. Houser, a Campo, Colorado, farmer, says that his low debt load and large operation will allow him to survive longer than most but that he still loses money on every crop he plants. "I'm going to see the handwriting on the wall," he declares, "and I'm not going to be here to read the last sentence."

The financial situation has darkened severely in recent years on the farm as a number of the statistics show. Net income was forecast in 1985 at barely half of 1979's level. Exports were forecast at 150 million metric tons in 1985, 14 million less than in 1980. Land prices have dropped from their peak average of $795 per acre in 1981 to less than $700 today. This means an erosion of collateral for much needed loans. Debts climbed from $60 billion in 1973 to $212 billion in 1985. These debts have slowed because farmers are running out of borrowing power just as the rest of the world's industry will soon be doing as we have already peaked in long-wave expansion.

Farms are going broke at rates not seen since the Great Depression due to the many pressures we have been discussing. The farms that survive these difficult times will take on many new characteristics in the coming years. These changes will be forced by financial necessities brought on by the pressures created by the long-wave forces at work. The farm must be forced to cut many of its strings with the government. There will always be room for the government to get involved in small ways with experimentation in crops and new procedures. However, the current extent of the marriage between the farm and Washington has to change drastically. Price supports and government props do nothing more than increase the inefficiencies in agriculture. There will be great pressure for more government in agriculture as things get worse but these pressures should be resisted as the free market is the best regulator in any industry. The worsening of the current decline will be an excellent opportunity to remove Washington from the farm by purging inefficiencies through failure.

It is interesting to hear the public and those who are in other industries say, "The farmer got himself in this situation let him get himself out." These same people will soon be caught in the same situation of falling prices and too much debt service to cover their expenses. They will see the value of their collateral eroded so that their plea for working capital at the local bank will fall on deaf ears and it will be their turn to march on Washington.

There is, no doubt, a time coming when the farmer will be given far more sympathy than he is being allotted today. Senate Republican Alan Simpson of Wyoming, speaking on the farm crisis, let it be known very clearly that the party cannot last forever when he said, "Somewhere along the line, there will be a moment of truth in this country. We're coming into it and it will be across the board at every level."

The trouble on the farm has in no way left the rest of the economy unscathed, especially in areas directly affected by the farm economy. One such area is the banking industry, which has suffered greatly over the past few years and will no doubt suffer far more in the coming years due to the uncollectible loans lent to the farmers during the good old days of the 60s and 70s.

The government-backed Farm Credit System has gotten itself deep into trouble and as of yet there is no light at the end of the tunnel. Rural banks are dropping like flies in the Midwest and the amount of failures is still on the increase. The Farmers Home Administration is deteriorating at a rapid pace with delinquent loans reaching astronomical proportion. The Federal Deposit Insurance Corporation is having trouble staying in the black with the enormous number of insured bank failures due to the farming crisis. The question arises: How much more pressure can the banking system take in consideration of the Third World pressures and energy-loan pressures coupled with the farming crisis? What is going to happen when the rest of the economy begins to get into trouble?

The banks are not the only businesses being affected by the farm crisis. The stores on Main Street in farming communities all across America are beginning to feel the pain of the farmer. As the farmer is pinched for cash, so is every store that depends on his business. The U.S. farm-equipment industry is operating at less than 50 percent of capacity and grain exporters are operating at less than 60 percent capacity. So the farmer is not the only one hurting during this time of sliding land values and falling prices. Farm-related businesses are getting a glimpse of things to come as the world stands casually observing.

There is no doubt that agriculture will go through major changes in the coming years of economic decline. However, new inventions and genetic breakthroughs coupled with more efficient computerized machinery will bring agriculture out of the decline before the rest of the economy. As we enter the 21st century, agriculture will once again be seen as a priority and not an expendable part of the economy. The planet earth could well be populated with over 6 billion people by the year 2,000 and the only industry that can feed them is agriculture.

Seely G. Lodwick, who is former under secretary of agriculture for International Affairs and Commodity Programs, has some insightful ideas on the direction of U.S. agriculture in the years to come: "The other certainty, along with taxes, is that the world's people will want to eat better than they have in the past. Those who are hungry and malnourished want to have adequate diets and the world must find ways to meet that need. Those people with only adequate diets want to have food that is more nutritious, more varied, richer in protein. Not only do they want more protein in their diets, they need it. As developing countries increase their consumption of poultry, dairy and livestock products, their people become stronger, healthier and longer lived — more capable of contributing to the advancement and development of their countries and ours too. We can no longer afford to squander the energy and talent that are lost in people who cannot fully perform because they are not well fed.

The problems of the world are too numerous and too large and we need the capabilities of all the world's people. This invites innovation on the part of American farmers and traders to find ways of serving those needs. We have the opportunity to expand exports of processed foods and other high-value products that increase dollar returns to this country and also create non-farm jobs in processing and food manufacturing. We also have the challenge to find new methods of trading — barter and counter-trade, for example — and the linking of trade with development projects that make imports possible for the poorer countries. All this adds up to a growth opportunity for those Americans who produce food. Food producers will be the key to progress towards a future world of peace and plenty."

The old proverb, "The only thing that is permanent is change," comes to mind as we observe agriculture moving through the long-wave cycle. Even though farms are faced once again in the peak of the long wave with high real interest rates, rising protectionism, falling land and commodity prices and rising operating costs, we must look beyond the current situation to the next advance of the long wave and realize that once again agriculture will come into its own but as a more efficient, better organized system that will face the rising problem of an exploding world population.

Without the pain that forces drastic innovation and new ideas and solutions to the world's problems, we would not be as advanced nor would we have many of the things today that make life far more pleasant and enjoyable than ever before.

I am sure during these hard times many are wishing for the "good old days on the farm," but there is really no more exciting time to be alive than when the world is going through major changes. The years to come on the farm, as we pull out of the coming decline, will be very rewarding and fascinating times to be involved in agriculture and many will be saying, "We never had it so good."

We must remember as we struggle through the coming decline that the darkest hour is just before the dawn; so it is on the farm.

10

Technology and Invention

Kondratieff began his review of long-wave theory by stressing that capitalist economies progress in a cyclical pattern rather than in a linear or constantly advancing manner. This cyclical pattern is always progressing in an upward trend and each new cycle of the long wave starts out further along in the development of the world economy and the advance of civilization than did the preceding advance.

The development of technology and the introduction of new inventions play a major role in the character of the long-wave cycle. If it were not for innovation, the long wave would just continue to turn over in one place and society would make no real progress towards improved living conditions and better ways of doing things.

Innovation also increases efficiencies in the world marketplace. Chapter Four touched on the fact that the constant movement towards a more closely linked world system is greatly encouraged by new technology. When and how the new technology is introduced and capitalized plays a major role in the rise and fall of the long-wave cycle.

Where would the world be without the invention of the internal combustion engine, which changed the way the world does business? Consider the impact of the airplane on the way the world has become interrelated and linked in all areas of commerce. Everything from the wheel to the computer has helped economic development and there is no sign of a slowdown in ideas and new ways to tackle the world's problems. This includes everything from simply feeding people to building permanent space colonies. Great advances are being made in genetic engineering that will maximize food output and help us to feed the growing world population. We are moving by leaps and bounds in technology towards living and working in outer space.

So how does it all relate to the long-wave cycle? There has

been a great deal of speculation and discussion on just how new inventions and technology contribute to the rise and fall of the economy. Kondratieff's research attempted to show that there was an increase of inventions during a decline because people were looking for more efficient and effective ways of production to get their particular industry moving in a profitable direction. Kondratieff emphasized heavily the effect of inventions in the areas of communications and transportation on the long wave.

This is extremely interesting in that as we come out of a decline these two areas are directly related to the growing strength and trend towards a world economy. There are a number of conclusions one could come to in trying to understand why inventions increase during a decline. Of course there is the possibility that during hard times man tends to be more of a thinking and contemplative creature and thus spends more time considering his predicament and how he intends to better his condition. This would naturally lead to an increase in the imaginative processes of the human mind and would in turn lead to ideas and inventions to solve the problems that man is facing.

It is extremely difficult to study the effect of invention on the long wave due to the complexity of both the inventing process and the implementation of new ideas. The problem with just totalling the number of inventions during the decline and comparing it to the total during the upswing is that inventions have different qualities and characteristics and fall into different categories of interpretation. Some inventions are in the capital goods area which are developed in an effort to minimize the cost of producing consumer products and are usually developed in research and development departments of industry and government. Other inventions are in the area of consumer goods and new retail products aimed at improving the life of the general public rather than efficiency in industry. These inventions come from both the private sector (the freelance inventor) and the R & D of industry.

For the past 200 years, there has been a steady increase in the number of inventions each year while it would seem through the research of a number of individuals, including Kondratieff, that some of the more important inventions that had enormous economic impact were developed during the major economic declines in history.

Gerhard Mensch assembled important evidence that clusters of basic innovations occurred in the 1820s, the 1880s and the 1930s, exactly during stagnating long waves. Economic history,

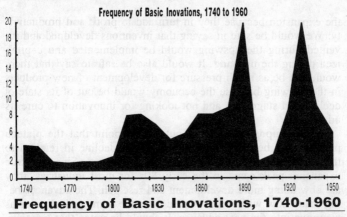

Frequency of Basic Inovations, 1740 to 1960

Frequency of Basic Inovations, 1740-1960

in turn, confirms that the investment outlays for the first massive applications of these basic innovations generally occurred 10 years later, after the turn from the depressive long wave to the expansionist long wave had already taken place. The included graph shows the relationship which Mensch discovered.

It would seem that the time of invention is not as important to understanding the dynamics of long waves as is an understanding of the economic forces at work which cause capital to flow into the new innovations so that they are integrated into the next upswing of growth and expansion.

J. Schmookler, as pointed out by Mandel, "has tried to prove that the patent cycle is closely related to the business cycle in general and does not precede or anticipate it."

This is to say that inventions will increase with the advance of the long wave and decrease with the decline of the long wave.

Mandel continues, "Although the argumentation seems convincing, it does not distinguish between qualitatively different types of patents and thus it cannot provide an answer to the question we pose. What is decisive is the phenomenon of patents permitting radical innovations, not the patent cycle in general."

Although inventing is going on both during the advance as well as the decline, it is obvious that these inventions are going to be utilized far more when industry can afford it, which is as profits begin to increase moving into the long-wave advance.

Lower interest rates and wages as well as cheaper raw materials greatly increase the profit picture thus creating more investment capital for implementation of new technology. The implementation of these inventions has a snowballing effect on the expansion because they in turn add to profit and productivity. We would be safe in saying that inventions developed and invented during the upswing would be implemented and capitalized during the upswing. It would also be safe to say that there would not be as much pressure for development of new products in the upswing because the economy would be out of its state of decline and stagnation and not looking for innovation to cure its ailments.

It is important to point out at this point that the plateau period could be considered as part of the decline in relation to the development and innovation of new products. Since the true expansion peak came in the early 80s for most industries, they are now doing more development and research. The advances being made now will be introduced after the coming decline or as we move into the next advance. It should be noted that a majority of the new developments will come after we fall off the plateau and enter the decline.

This has been the case in all long-wave declines of the past. However, it is clear that a great many advances can be made during the plateau that are important to the forward march of technology and science.

As the long-wave peaks in the financial markets and we come to the end of the plateau and enter the decline, industry will begin to get caught in the same squeeze that has been plaguing agriculture for 10 years. The slow-down of investment in expansion will be profound. When the general overexpansion and overcapitalization of industry with expensive debt begins to take its toll and the buying power of the world is eroded then prices begin to tumble. As prices fall below what it cost to produce, the screws will tighten on the economy.

For a while companies will still operate to cover fixed cost but soon prices will drop too far and companies will begin to shut their doors. Unemployment and bankruptcies will reach new highs with every passing day and the entire economy will slow substantially. As we move deeper into the decline and companies are no longer expanding, that is the ones which make it through the first years of the decline, there begins to be a build-up of capital. Interest rates, wages and payrolls are falling during the decline so the profit picture begins to improve, yet companies with their new-found tendencies towards risk aversion are extremely slow to expand or spend money on major outlays.

A natural place for the investment of the companies excess

capital during this time is in the R&D departments. This new research expenditure coupled with the psychological factors of looking for solutions during hard times breeds new products that can help pull the world out of its economic slumber and into the next upswing of the cycle. This is true in the long wave but could be applied as well to the seven-to-11-year cycle which attains a great deal of its character from the long wave within which it exists. The times of economic expansion and contraction in the intermediate cycle would, as in the case of the long wave, lend themselves to research during contraction and implementation during expansion.

As pointed out earlier, Kondratieff concentrated heavily on inventions in transportation and communications and their impact on the next expansion in the long wave. Transportation and communication are extremely important fields of development in that they have a double effect on a growth economy during the expansion period of the long wave. First they create new industries of their own in the way of investment and profit. This has been the case within the fields of electronics, telecommunications, airlines, shipping, railroads and satellites. These have become enormous industries composed of hundreds of thousands of companies which employ millions of people and stimulate billions of dollars in the economy.

Secondly these companies generate more trade among nations and continents and in effect stimulate the development of the world economy. This stimulus to world trade helps to encourage development and capitalization of new inventions and products that are not necessarily in the fields of communications or transportation. We are all aware of all the major communications and transportation inventions including the telephone, telegraph, automobile, train, airplane, satellite, subway, television, radio, computer and oil tanker, to name only a few of the many inventions which have shaped the destinies of nations with their impact on the world economy. What is not so evident is that these inventions led to the widespread use of all other inventions in the international marketplace.

The act of inventing and the process of development and implementation of inventions is all part of what we consider the growth of technology. It is said that man is now doubling his knowledge of the universe every few years. This increase in knowledge and the explosion of technology that accompanies it is opening all sorts of avenues for business and science. These new avenues are creating wonderful opportunities to build a bet-

ter world and are providing for the possibility of a more peaceful co-existence among nations.

There is, of course, the more negative side in that we must
acknowledge that technology has also opened the door to the potential total destruction of the world as we know it. This problem should be addressed but not with misguided idealism that
will only increase tension. We will address these unfortunate
issues in more detail later.

What one doesn't notice readily is the impact this technological advance is having on the Kondratieff long wave and how
it is playing a major role in shaping the emergence of our world
community and marketplace.

Chapter Four touched briefly on the technological impact
on our world community but I would like to discuss it a bit
further at this point.

The vast network that has been created through the new
technology in communications which links every corner of the
world through an electrical impulse could be viewed as the central nervous system to the world economy. The impact of this
system has yet to be fully realized by its millions of users every
day. Even though few of us would like to admit it, the international monetary system is the major player in how the world
economy is functioning. With the conflict in exchange rates, the
pitiful condition of the economies of the Third World and the
unstable condition of the international banking system, we are
beginning to hear cries for a new monetary system. The fact of
the matter is that we already have a new monetary system which
owes its life to innovation and new technology in the communications industry. Walter Wriston, former chairman for Citicorp,
discussed this new system in a column in *The Wall Street Journal* on November 12, 1985.

This example is to be a brief illustration of the enormous
impact of invention on the world economy and marketplace today:

> *The new system was not built by politicians or econo-
> mists. It was built by technology. In some respects the new
> world financial system is the accidental by-product of com-
> munication satellites and of engineers learning how to use
> the electromagnet spectrum up to 300 gigahertz. In the same
> manner that Edison failed to foresee that his phonograph
> would have any commercial value, the men and women who
> tied the world together with telecommunications did not fully
> realize that they were building the infrastructure of a world
> marketplace.*

The convergence of computers with telecommunications has produced a world trading system, which in turn has allowed creation of a new international monetary system I call the Information Standard. Because this world market is something different in kind and not just a change in degree, it has truly revolutionized the world. Political, regulatory and economic concepts and compacts suddenly lose some of their relevance and everyone from business people to politicians has new issues to worry about. The new Information Standard, unlike all prior arrangements, is not subject to effective political tinkering ...

Prior to the advent of the Information Standard, if a country did not like the gold standard or the gold exchange standard or the Bretton Woods arrangement, it could opt out of the system. A finance minister would call a press conference and explain that the current international arrangements were unsatisfactory and that his nation would no longer play. This was the fate of the gold exchange standard and the Bretton Woods fixed exchange standard. Today, there is no way for a nation to opt out of the Information Standard. There is no place on this planet to hide.

This massive reordering of the international financial system has been largely overlooked because the scientists who created the technology did not focus on their creation of the world marketplace and the central bankers and governments weren't trained to anticipate the impact of technology on currency values. But ready or not, the technology won't go away, the market won't stop making judgments every minute and the Information Standard is here. Like other forms of free speech, government will have to learn to live with it.

Wriston is extremely accurate in his interpretation of the character of our new monetary system, but he fails to see the even more dramatic changes that will occur. What he has described is the hardware to the emerging new system.

We have yet to see the software package which will be introduced as the solution to the coming financial collapse. There is no doubt in the minds of most that there is a day of reckoning coming in international financial markets and there will invariably be a collapse of the current banking system.

The new banking system that will emerge as a result of the collapse will fit nicely with the new international monetary system and will be much more effective and efficient for international development and strengthening of the world economic community. The existing banking order is sitting on edge in fear of the next economic slowdown that will no doubt push it over the edge.

In review of the impact of invention and technology, we see they play a vital yet not easily perceived role in the economic expansion and contraction of the long wave. The evidence of innovation stimulating the advance, especially in the areas of communications and technology, only becomes clear as we examine closely the growth in capital outlays and the use of new inventions in generating accelerated profit rates as the long wave swings into its advance. In considering this impact it would perhaps be enlightening to look to the future and try to make an educated guess at what new developments and products will stimulate the next advance of the long wave.

As Kondratieff and others have explained and as we have seen in this chapter, communications and transportation are the leaders in pulling the economy out of the contraction and into the expansion. As we anticipate the sharp economic decline of the long wave in the near future it would be interesting to look ahead to the potential innovations that will pull us out of the contraction and into the next economic expansion. The next decline will be short as was the Great Depression, relative to the long-wave declines of the past. Because of the shortened decline, the next advance will begin in the mid- to late 90s.

Consider the enormous impact of the space shuttle and other space advances which fall into the innovation category of transportation and which is accompanied by great breakthroughs in communications. The tragedy of the *Challenger* shuttle will only prove to be a minor setback and slowdown for the race for space and could prove to force us into better design and ultimately quicker implementation of new, more advanced systems. One such development could well be a space plane that will take off horizontally. We will see great advances and enormous amounts of development in all areas of space in the early 90s which will help lead the world economy into the next advance.

The Saturday Evening Post ran an article in the March, 1985 issue entitled, "American Business: Heading Into Orbit." In this article Arthur M. Dula and Ann Zeigler speculated as to what the future holds in the way of economic expansion into space. This is only one more example of the great impact of technology and innovation on the economy.

They wrote:

> *Scientists and corporate planners are working hard on blueprints for space industries that will employ thousands and earn billions ... The American Lunar Base Luna in Cayley Crater, could be in operation in the year 2000, a mere 15 years from now. In 1977 a NASA study proposed the Cayley*

base as an example of how people could live and work in Luna. In October 1984 more than 100 NASA and university scientists met in Washington to plan how Luna will become the research and commercial center of space industry ... The McDonnell Douglas Corporation has estimated that the 1984-94 space-market size will reach $10-$20 billion for communications, $1 billion for remote sensing, $20-$40 billion for materials and manufacturing and $4-$6 billion for orbital transport services. Rep. D.K. Akaka of Hawaii, founder of the 164-member, bipartisan Congressional Space Caucus, has estimated that commercial space activity may be worth as much as $200-$300 billion to our national economy by 2,000 and may create as many as 10 million jobs over the next decade. Rep. Robert S. Walker of Pennsylvania agrees. He believes the United States should commit itself to a goal of building a $500 billion space economy to generate 20 million new jobs by the end of the century ...

Can't we manufacture goods perfectly well down here for less? Not really. Abundant solar energy, microgravity and pure vacuum mean new types of pure drugs, large, perfect crystals and new metal alloys can be produced in space and on the moon. The moon is a source of the most necessary item in space travel-fuel. (Liquid oxygen used as fuel is a significant part of the cargo now carried by the space shuttle). The lunar rocks our astronauts brought home have turned out to be about half oxygen. If we can get to the moon and set up lunar mining outposts, we can produce vast quantities of oxygen to fuel space travel, space stations, space colonies, space farms and space factories ... A study by General Dynamics for NASA predicts that up to 90 percent of the material used in space structures can be obtained by mining the moon ... The Soviet Union has estimated the economic impact of "extraterrestrial industry" and space manufacturing to be $50 billion as early as 1990. To encourage this expansion of the Soviet economic frontier, the Soviets are developing a launch vehicle capable of carrying from 200 to 400 tons into space — 10 to 20 times the payload of the space shuttle. The Soviets are planning a "Kosmograd" space base for the late 1980s. The base will have several hundred inhabitants and will lead to a Soviet lunar base; the government is already training 300 of its brightest children in Moscow at a special school for space colonists. Public and private, big and small, East and West — people are preparing to do business in space. Just as our forefathers followed the sun and the winds in search of a better life, so we and our children are following the sun's rays back toward their source and beyond."

Space is only one area that will see enormous advances during the next expansive upswing of the long wave. Biotechnology and genetic engineering will open new frontiers for industry. Artificial intelligence and the use of robots will bring numerous avenues of growth to the economy.

First we face the decline during which the impurities and inefficiencies that have built up over the past 50 years, such as excessive interest rates, debt and outrageous wages in many industries will be purged from the system. The result will be a more centralized, innovative, prospering, efficient and expanding world economy.

Looking back over the evidence of this chapter we see that technology and invention do indeed play a major role in the rise and fall of the long-wave cycle.

11

On Politics

There has been a great deal of debate over the centuries as to which force is more dominate in molding the destiny of man, economics or politics. In relation to the Kondratieff Wave in Western nations, there is no doubt that the location of the economy within the wave has great impact on what sort of political rhetoric or ideology will get you elected.

Few would argue that what gave Franklin Roosevelt victory in 1932 was the pain of the Great Depression and his promise that government would take care of the people and bring industry under control. His promise to more closely regulate the banking industry and the markets, which were perceived as catalysts of the crash in 1929, served as major factors as well.

By the same token, few would question that Ronald Reagan's promise to get government off people's backs and to give industry more freedom in the marketplace through deregulation played a large role in his being elected in 1980 and reelected in 1984.

Why two totally different positions, across the board and victory in both cases? There should be no doubt that the location of the economy within the long wave and its impact in all areas of life is the chief reason for such different platforms yielding the same result — victory.

This line of thought would lead us to the conclusion of the old question of supremacy between politics and economics. In view of long-wave realities, we have to hail economics as king. It would be foolish to try and link every president from George Washington to Reagan with the position of the economy relative to the long-wave cycle. Long-wave theory does not attempt to do so. It is, however, possible to make such a link during the critical "peaks" of the long wave. These prove to be the most volatile periods for the economy and thus the most predictable periods in the struggle for power within the political system.

There are powerful forces at work in the years leading up to the peak as well as the first few years as the economy moves or crashes into the decline. The politically liberal party scarcely has a chance for victory as we move into the prosperous *laissez-faire* climate in the last few years of the upswing. The conservative party hasn't a prayer when the economy comes crashing down and the shortsighted public perceives the decline as the incompetent policy and the *laissez-faire*, deregulation of the current administration.

These are some interesting conclusions in light of the current position in which we find ourselves. We are once again on the plateau and approaching the decline of the long wave. This current expansion of the intermediate seven-to-11-year cycle should peak at any time at which point we will also see the market peak of the long wave. The economy will then turn into a sharp decline for a number of years. This would lead us to the conclusion that a conservative Republican would be elected in 1988 if the economy is healthy, and 1992 will see a sweeping victory for the liberal Democratic party.

If the economy doesn't collapse early, then the 1988 elections will no doubt see another Republican president and administration as the economy should be doing extremely well. Robert Dole or George Bush are perhaps the most likely possibilities but Jack Kemp should keep them looking over their shoulders and Pat Robertson will no doubt give a far more powerful showing than anyone would imagine — if he decides to run. Robertson is a student of the Kondratieff long wave and is very much aware of the powerful forces it generates. The conservative grass-roots reaction to the liberal social trends we see in the plateau of the long wave will give Robertson far more viability than most would anticipate.

As we discussed briefly in Chapter Five on the psychology of the wave, the religious revival we will see as we enter the decline could give a Republican president with religious foundations an excellent chance at re-election in 1992.

He would of course first face the great difficulty of having to win in 1988. A Republican without a religious appeal will have a very difficult-to-impossible time of it trying to stay in power in 1992. There is, of course, an outside chance a Democrat could win office in 1988 but this is highly unlikely. If a Democrat does happen to win in 1988, this shouldn't change one's belief in the long-wave cycle. The only change a Democratic victory in 1988 would make is that it would be the party that gets blamed for causing the coming collapse and depression.

What sort of man will come to power in 1992 if we do see a shift from conservative to liberal politics and the Democratic party? He will no doubt be a man from a family with a household name and with considerable ties and background to the Democratic party. New names and faces don't sit well with a nation in crisis. Not that I approve but the name Kennedy will have a powerful ring to it as this nation looks for something to hold on to. Sen. Edward Kennedy would do well to take notice of the flow of the long-wave cycle as it takes everything, including the hearts of the electorate, in its path.

The long-wave will have an enormous impact on political and economic leadership as we get over the initial shock of the decline and the reactionary move towards politically liberal leaders such as Kennedy.

As we have discussed in depth, the new cycle always leads towards a more centralized international world and economy and there will be a tremendous need for leaders with a truly international background and education in the coming years.

Ronald Reagan has been an excellent domestic president while his foreign policy has been determined by persons other than himself. The Reagan administration, as well as past administrations, has failed to perceive the true issues and problems facing the United States and the Western world in the international economic arena.

The United States has no long-range foreign policy goals or objectives and is caught reacting to Eastern Bloc policy rather than establishing well-thought-out policy of its own. What we have lacked is a stable, well-thought-out agenda that would lead to consistent decisions in the best political and economic interest of the Western world.

Since World War II United States foreign policy has been nothing more than reactionary. This policy has always led to unnecessary embarrassment that has been costly both in dollar amounts as well as exacting a heavy toll in human life. We get ourselves into situations which could have been avoided with long-range planning and we are forced to blunder our way out at great cost to our international reputation.

The Soviet Union is no less than thrilled with our East-West stance on every issue. This stance gives them prestige and importance which their failing system does not deserve. Soviet aggression is to be feared and their aggressive behavior in Eastern Europe at the close of World War II is a large reason for the emergence of the East-West view that dominates United States foreign policy today. A majority of us do not have any false perceptions as to what Soviet intentions are. President Reagan's perception of the Soviet Union as "The Evil Empire" is no doubt accurate — at least as far as the leadership of the Soviet Union is concerned. The common citizen in the Soviet Union would be little different than his American counterpart.

A great majority of the current problems in the world that the United States has been or will invariably be drawn into can be traced back 30 or 40 years to the need for long-range vision in international economic policy. If government leaders and the powerful corporate individuals, who determined government and corporate policy during the first few years of the post-colonial period following World War II, had had more long-range vision there is no doubt that Cuba, Nicaragua, Angola, Ethiopia and many other Third World nations would be democratic states today and would be profitable areas of investment for western capital. If long-range objectives had guided decisions in past decades the world would be a much safer and more pleasant place to live and do business today. We should not fall into the simplistic trap of linking all problems in developing nations to the course of economics.

There were of course strong internal and external political pressures that exploded for non-economic reasons in many nations. Soviet expansionism was no doubt one of the major problems and still is today. But to limit our vision of the problems to nothing more than a Soviet threat would be foolish. There are real economic problems in many of the hot spots around the world and there are varying degrees of economic exploitation throughout the world that cannot be denied.

Our reactionary policy that looks at the world through East-West colored glasses has, on many occasions, led the United States into the arms of the leading group or person in a Third World nation that shouted anti-communist rhetoric the loudest. It is certainly noble to take a pro-free market and anti-communist stance and more Americans should do so but to have this ideal as the center of policy decision making is dangerous.

The Reagan administration has a far better record than preceding administrations in understanding the foolishness of such a policy. East-West foreign policy has, on a number of occasions, led the United States into alliances and treaties with ruthless right-wing regimes that are no better than the communism they claim to fight against and prevent. These regimes have often suppressed values we Americans hold dearest and have fought principles which were the foundations of our own fight for independence. Obviously I wholeheartedly support the free-market system but it must be a system that has its own long-term best interest in mind. This might not always be equated with short-term profit. We need to be willing to support change.

Being a generally conservative nation we often fear change and because of this we have supported leaders who guarantee the maintenance of the *status quo*. The *status quo* is often the problem and change is what we need — as we saw in the Philippines. No one is under the false impression that change can come all at once in any nation or region. However, we do realize that it must come if these regions are to survive as friendly to the United States and Western interests.

The United States needs to have a foreign policy that seeks to establish and grant to the people of the world the same general rights granted to her own people in her own constitution. Why should the people of the world expect anything less? A long-range foreign policy would of course be more complex than this may sound and I am not saying there is a simple answer. It should be understood by any leader or nation seeking to deal with the United States, whether economically or politically, that we stand firm in our constitutional convictions and are willing to enforce those convictions with our economic and military strength. The Soviet Union's economic system is failing under even the lowest of standards and we shouldn't act as if they are our competition.

The multi-national corporation must begin to acknowledge the forces at work in the international arena. They cannot stop these forces but can use them to their own long-term advantage instead of falling into the trap of sowing the seeds of their own destruction for nothing more than passing short-term profits. The multi-national giants are far more long-term conscious than the old corporations that were closely held and run by family members who couldn't see beyond a few years. They certainly couldn't see the revolutionary spirit that would sweep the Third World and destroy the companies that sought to do business in those areas.

The CEOs of the big multi-national companies are well aware that a few policy changes and reforms now could save whole foreign divisions in the future. The large multi-national is a living entity that intends to carry on long after the current board and executives are gone. This lends itself to more long-term rational decision making. The United States' foreign policy coupled with long-range corporate objectives of the multi-national could be a powerful force in bringing stability to the world — especially the Third World.

In some areas time has run out and military solutions will have to be used to solve the problems. In most areas there is still time for reform that will grant a sound future for the profits of the multi-national if only they will work together with a United States foreign policy that will seek long-term goals and objectives.

The Soviets certainly have long-term goals with plans and strategies to fulfill their objectives. Why shouldn't the United States be just as committed to long-term foreign policy and objectives that offer help to a hurting world, instead of our throwing fuel on the enemy's fire.

There has been a glimmer of hope in recent months as we have seen our foreign policy demand democracy in the Philippines and Haiti instead of anti-communist rhetoric. It was the sign of a real change towards long-range planning to see the Reagan administration support the fall of both Duvalier and Marcos in an effort to encourage more stable democratic governments in those two nations. These changes in policy will go further than anyone would ever have imagined possible to rid the world of the political and economic cancer of communism. The world does not need any more rhetoric, it needs economic and political action that will undermine communist intentions.

Another important element to the long-wave cycle is that we are seeing a resurgence of nationalism all over the world, in every nation. This is a healthy and good thing in and of itself but there is a danger of it becoming economic isolationism. This isolationism is threatening the life of the world economy and could possibly cause the coming decline to be far more lengthy and devastating than it has to be. The United States will be in dire need of leaders who can stimulate great domestic faith while at the same time deal in an insightful and meaningful way with the forces at work in the international environment. This will be true of every nation in the international arena where such men will no doubt be in short supply.

The new nationalism we have seen emerging deserves a closer look as we consider its impact on the coming long-wave decline and the following long-wave expansion of the economy. Since World War II the world has moved into the post-colonial period. Africa, the Middle East and Asia have all gained independence from Western dominance of their political systems.

This has led to a new type of international environment. Many of these nations have been in a dilemma since finding their independence because they are being forced to choose between East and West political alliance. This has caused a great deal of confusion on the part of most of these nations who have enough problems just meeting the basic needs for survival. The governments of the Third World are too concerned with putting food on the table and carving out a better life for their people to spend all their time and energy on an East-West conflict. The East-West decision helped cause this turn inward and intense resurgence in nationalism that is often at the expense of economic realities that demand movement towards increased international trade and foreign relationships.

The United States is a great enough power not to demand verbal allegiance. We should earn the allegiance of Third World nations by supporting economic growth and recovery with fair and just treatment for the people of these nations. These nations should be allowed to be nationalistic and supportive of their governments. As we have entered the plateau of the long wave this nationalism has had a tendency to encourage protectionism in the illusion that protectionism keeps a nation from harmful outside competition.

In reality, international associations and outside competition help to stimulate trade and help expansion and growth of the nation's economy in the long run.

This new wave of nationalism has been powerful in the United States as in the rest of the world and has been a positive thing by giving us a new pride in quality and a job well done. At the same time this nationalism has led us down the dead-end road of protectionism and economic isolationism. There will no doubt be enormous pressure for the world's new nationalism to bring increased economic isolation as the economy moves into the coming decline. We will need leaders who can convince their people with authority that this is not the road to take. Increased economic isolation could make the coming decline shadow the Great Depression in its severity.

We should fight economic isolationism across the board and at every level. A nation can believe in itself politically without shutting its doors to foreign competition. Nationalism must be used to increase productivity in a world economy whose nations are in healthy economic competition with one another.

12

Preparing for Depression

The reader is aware that on Oct. 19, 1987, the Dow Jones industrial average plunged 508 points — over 22 percent of the market value, dwarfing the better than 12 percent collapse of Oct. 28, 1929.

Part III:
The Intelligent
Investor

The market then stabilized a bit. It is probable that this break in the market is the beginning of the long-awaited collapse in financial markets, brought on by the forces at work in the long-wave cycle.

Due to the speed technology has brought to the marketplace, there is also the possibility that this is a massive correction. This cataclysmic drop could have been overdone by computers. There is a chance we will pull out of this and thus head to higher ground before the total collapse.

But at present the indicators do not point to recovery. I am hoping for more time to prepare individuals for what lies ahead but perhaps that is only wishful thinking. Time is now of the essence.

The long-wave cycle is a 50-to 60-year cycle and deals with the fundamentals in the financial markets and economy. The long-wave cycle does not lend itself to market timing and I do not claim to be a market timer. The evidence of long-wave theory says that we are or were in the plateau and headed for a major market collapse that will push us into a world wide economic depression.

There will be great danger if we pull out of this recent market collapse as most will then think the market and the system is invincible. If we pull out of this then the crash, when it does come, will make Oct. 19, 1987 look like a Sunday afternoon picnic. At present it is unlikely that we will recover from this downturn.

125

is important at this point to look back to 1929. After the collapse on Oct. 28, 1929 and the subsequent drop the following day the market came back with a vengeance for several days — far more than the markets regained in the first days following the recent crash of 1987. Yet today like in 1929 this caused individuals and institutions to hold out hope that the market would rebound from its slide. For months after the collapse in 1929 the market in fact came back and even gained substantial ground. But the damage had already been done — the back of market psychology had been snapped. As is taking place again today we were slowly moving from a universal disposition of optimism to one of intense pessimism.

We have already begun to see a retrenchment in consumer spending across the board. The important point is that this slow down, and I might add a slow down that will accelerate, is occurring in the plateau of the long-wave cycle. Almost every industry in the world is overproducing and doing so with expensive debt. The individuals, corporations and governments of the world are deep in debt and will soon slam on the brakes — sending the world economy over the edge and into the deepest depression the world has ever seen.

We are currently approaching $9 trillion of total debt in the United States. Anyone who believes that a major pull back in spending at this time will not bring the economy to its knees is living a life of illusion. The roaring eighties are quickly coming to an abrupt end.

The purpose of this book is to inform the reader as to why current events are taking place in the economy and the financial markets and to assist the reader in preparing for the coming years. As pointed out I first thought we would have more time to prepare for the crash and depression but it would appear the clock is now ticking and time is running short.

This chapter is an attempt to present the reader with some rough guidelines in preparing for a depression. Please remember that if we pull out of the current down turn by some stroke of free-market luck then the reckoning has only been postponed. The reader should be prepared rather than foolishly hoping for the best.

The very first consideration for anyone preparing for the coming depression is to get out of debt. This is of extreme importance. We are on the edge of a deflationary depression that will make all debt drastically more expensive. This goes for credit cards, automobiles and houses as well as personal loans. Getting out of debt is a tall order but one that should be filled if at all possible.

Credit cards can be useful if they are used only for convenience and paid off every month. Otherwise they should not be used. Many have savings or investments that could be used to pay down debts and this should be done immediately. Most are not able to pay off the mortgage on their homes and do not want to sell their homes. One consideration would be to go to a variable rate mortgage. During a deflationary collapse interest rates will collapse and so will your mortgage payment — if it is variable and pegged to the T-Bill rate or federal funds rate. Try to get your banker to drop any floor in the mortgage contract. If necessary you should consider selling any assets you could bear to part with in order to pay off debts.

Another all important point is to stop spending yourself into oblivion. Put a hold on any and all purchases that are not totally necessary. That new washer and dryer can wait. Take all extra income and save it or pay off existing debt. It is high time we all began living within our means. After paying off as many debts as possible and curtailing spending it is time to look for a safe bank.

Just like 1929 the market collapse leads us into a depression of such magnitude that the banking system begins to weaken drastically. It was 1931 when banking failures reached their peak the last time around as failures soared. Even prudent savers were wiped out by unprecedented failures in the banking industry. Now is the time to begin shifting your assets and cash to safe banks. You would not want to be caught in a weak bank during the next few years.

Bank Valuation is a company based in New York that rates banks according to depositors' safety. Their research is done primarily for institutions but they may soon begin a smaller condensed version for individuals. Neill Reilly is the managing director and has agreed to allow me to publish a listing of the safest banks in the country. Bank Valuation composes two important analyses. One is the 150 largest banks by assets in the country and the other is the 50 largest banks by assets in the country. The approach BV uses is sound and the banks at the top of their lists will survive even the most severe depression and banking collapse. Bank Valuation releases their reports quarterly. The latest analysis on the 50 largest banks is the second quarter of 1987 while the 150 largest banks report comes from the first quarter of 1987. I will list the top 15 from the 150-bank report and the top 10 from the 50-bank report.

TOP 15 OF THE 150 LARGEST
BANKS IN THE COUNTRY

1st Quarter 1987

1. First-Citizens Bank & Trust Company,
   Raleigh, North Carolina.
2. First Union National Bank of Florida,
   Jacksonville, Florida.
3. Citizens & Southern Bank of Florida,
   Forth Lauderdale, Florida.
4. Citizens and Southern National Bank of
   South Carolina,
   Charleston, South Carolina.
5. Norstar Bank of Upstate New York,
   Albany, New York.
6. First Alabama Bank,
   Montgomery, Alabama.
7. First Union National Bank of North Carolina,
   Charlotte, North Carolina.
8. City National Bank,
   Beverly Hills, California.
9. Boston Safe Deposit & Trust Company,
   Boston, Massachusetts.
10. First Jersey National Bank,
    Jersey City, New Jersey.
11. BayBank Middlesex
    Burlington, Massachusetts.
12. Sovran Bank/Maryland,
    Bethesda, Maryland.
13. First Florida Bank,
    Tampa, Florida.
14. Equitable Bank,
    Baltimore, Maryland.
15. Central Bank of the South,
    Birmingham, Alabama.

TOP 10 OF 50 LARGEST BANKS
IN THE COUNTRY

2nd Quarter 1987

1. Wachovia Bank and Trust Company,
   Winston-Salem, North Carolina.
2. First Union National Bank of North Carolina,
   Charlotte, North Carolina.
3. Boston Safe Deposit and Trust Company
   Boston, Massachusetts
4. State Street Bank and Trust Company
   Boston, Massachusetts
5. United States National Bank of Oregon
   Portland, Oregon
6. National Bank of Detroit
   Detroit, Michigan
7. Maryland National Bank
   Baltimore, Maryland
8. Connecticut National Bank
   Hartford, Connecticut
9. Sovran Bank
   Richmond, Virginia
10. Comerica Bank-Detroit
    Detroit, Michigan

A portion of one's assets should be kept in cash as deposits or in certificates of deposit at one of these safe banking institutions — preferably with the ones closest to the top of the list. The amount of assets to be kept in cash will depend on the individuals' preferences and the amount of his assets. Never put all your eggs in one basket.

Once a safe bank has been located and the reader has shifted his liquid assets to this institution he then should closely look at the distribution of his assets among a number of protective positions. Although I do not look favorably at long-term government debt I believe short term government debt will make an excellent investment. By this I am referring to treasury bills. This is the government's short-term financing. Uncle Sam will have to keep the T-bill market liquid so that the government can function. The T-bill market is the government's bread and butter. The smallest denomination of a T-bill is $10,000 and can be bought directly from a Federal Reserve bank with no commission cost. If you cannot afford to buy in $10,000 blocks then there are a few mutual funds that invest purely in T-bills. By buying through a fund you can invest in smaller denominations of as little as 1,000. There are three solid funds that invest in T-bills. One of these funds is managed by United Services Funds and is the U.S. Treasury Securities Fund (800) 824-4653. Another company with a solid T-Bill fund is Neuberger & Berman Management Inc. and their fund is the Government Money Fund, Inc. (800) 367-0776. A third fund is managed by Benham Capital Management Group and is the Capital Preservation Fund, (800) 472-3389. These funds should make excellent investments for the coming years of depression but if possible I would recommend direct investment in T-bills in order to get around the funds. The fewer parties involved in your transactions the better.

Another position that all investors should consider moving into is gold. Gold investment should be in the form of actual gold as well as a few solid gold stocks or gold mutual funds. Dreyfus Precious Metals (800) 544-4424 is an excellent place to buy gold. They have very low commission prices and they will deliver insured gold coins or ingots to your bank to be deposited in your safety deposit box. The Canadian maple leaf is a great coin for investment.

There are a number of gold producing companies that are in strong financial positions. Gold stocks will be the only stocks that should be held during the coming depression. From 1929 to 1933 gold stocks gained 70 percent while other stocks lost 90 percent of their value. This was in an environment where gold was pegged to the dollar. This time around the free market will push gold to great heights and gold stocks may do far better than during the last depression. There is a great probability that we will see the emergence of a gold based monetary system during the coming depression. This will greatly enhance the price of gold and the value of gold shares. The following are a few gold companies that should make for excellent investments. These would be buy and hold investments until the mid-90s.

Newmont Mining Corporation
Homestake Mining Co.
Hecla Mining Co.
Callahan Mining Corporation
Battle Mountain

Other sound investments that are discussed later in this book will be bonds and debentures issued by AAA- and AA-rated companies. Look for bonds and debentures expiring between 1995 and 2000. Thirty-year debt that was issued from 1965 to 1970 and is selling at a discount would make the best investment. It may be difficult to find this quality debt but you should give it a shot. As you will read later debt-free real estate, although it will depreciate, should be a substantial portion of ones portfolio when possible.

Distribution of one's assets among the different protective positions will vary with the individual. It should go without saying that the time to prepare for the depression is now. You should take a close look, with the advice of an attorney, at the legal repercussions of a full scale depression on your debts and assets. There are a number of defensive moves that should be taken to protect yourself from hostile creditors. Only use an attorney that has experience in asset planning and banckruptcy. In light of recent market action I will leave you with a recent insightful observation by my savvy attorney Steven T. Aceto, "Once a rollercoaster has jumped the track I wouldn't rush to get back on board."

13

Stocks

The financial markets have long been the barometers of the world's business activity. As one begins to fully realize the great impact of the Kondratieff long wave on the economy, the question of its effect on stocks is usually the first to be addressed. Indeed it should be since the stock markets of the world hold the future to the lives of millions of people whose retirement and sustenance are dependent on the performance of mutual funds, pension funds and personal investments in stocks.

The carefully planned future of millions of people were radically changed in the great crash of 1929. Many are under the illusion that such a downturn could never happen again because of new rules and regulations such as increased margin requirements and close SEC regulation. Long-wave theory, with the weight of 200 years of history on its side, would tend to say such an occurrence is not only possible but highly probable.

The turn of the financial markets will mark the abrupt universal realization and acceptance that the world really is entering an economic decline which will last for some time to come. Many of those who only become aware of the coming economic decline as the market peaks and begins its descent will be seen jumping from the windows of tall buildings as they see all they have worked for crumbling down around them.

The mid-1920s, just like the late 1860s, are comparable economically in numerous ways with the present. There are underlying forces at work that cannot be fully realized unless a sweeping view of the economy is taken in. When we make this sweeping view, the landscape begins to look very familiar and the few who remember the roaring 20s begin to feel a cold chill running up their spines. Factories are scarcely using 80 percent of their capacity while shortages are virtually unknown.

World prices are beginning to sag and worries of oversupply are beginning to crop up. Production facilities are becoming obsolete and real capital expansion is slowing dramatically. National, corporate and individual debt is reaching levels that far surpass the levels of the late 20s. Something has got to give and give it will, according to my projections, by several thousand points.

In my chapter on psychology I briefly explored the generation gap and demonstrated that as old pessimistic blood is drained from the leadership in the economy, a new generation and breed of risk takers are taking over. The great pendulum of pain and pleasure has taken its rhythmic course and the pain is long forgotten. Taking precedence is the belief that the economy can only expand. This belief is most powerful as we enter the plateau of the long wave due to falling prices which control inflation and improving earnings which are due to the powerful elements affecting the economy generated by the long-wave cycle.

This was clearly seen in the 20s and many are beginning to see a distinct resemblance with the 80s. Certainly, everyone believes we will hit a pothole on occasion but no one really believes we could ever skid off the road. This creates a natural upward bias in stock markets based on what one could call the pendulum power of the generation gap. The upward momentum of the markets become somewhat of a sporting event and everyone truly wants to see the score get higher and higher. The only problem is that the forces and people driving the market are all on the same team, creating the illusion that everyone can be a winner.

I find a great deal of humor in the great variety of reasons that have been put forward for explanation of the bull markets of the past few years. One day it's interest rates, the next day it's earnings, then come falling oil prices. Sure, there are the intermediate cyclical conditions and the technical factors that all play an important role in the market but the most important and overriding element comes from the sweeping effect of the Kondratieff long wave as nothing, including the Dow Jones, escapes its path.

The forces driving the stock markets today are the same forces that were at work in the 1920s. On August 21, 1921, the Dow Jones Industrial Average was sitting at 63.90. In just over eight years, on September 3, 1929, the Dow hit 386.1. This height was not seen again for 25 years which was late in 1954. In the interim, the Dow bottomed at 40.56 on July 8, 1932.

Many would like to attribute the entire crash in the market to speculation and lenient rules and regulations. This of course was a factor but the forces at work that arise every 50 years or so had far more to do with the collapse than investors buying on margin. A recent article that quoted Robert Prechter and was discussing a potential crash in 1989 had exceptional insight into the foolishness of faith in today's margin requirements. The article said:

> Those hoping that any future collapse will be cushioned by post-1929 safeguards are misguided, Prechter says. Like fellow doomsayers James Grant and Jim Rogers, an investor, Prechter believes that today's 50 percent margin requirement, as opposed to 10 percent in 1929, offers only illusory protection. "These days," he says, "with options and futures and second mortgages, you can get much more than 10-to-one leverage. And at the top, people will be tremendously leveraged.

Although a great majority of people invested in the market in the late 20s were wiped out, there were a few astute investors who became quite wealthy during the period. There are a number of cases of people in high corporate positions whose companies and banks were boosting the market but who were personally selling out or going into short positions and thereby made vast fortunes while the rest of the world was in panic. There is no doubt the situation will be the same in the coming years.

As society becomes more and more affluent during an upswing and expansion, more people are able to invest in the markets with their increasing discretionary income. In the United States in 1952 there were only 6.5 million Americans who owned stock which was close to one in 20 of the population. By 1985 this number had grown to 47 million or one in five.

There is no doubt these numbers will increase as the public rushes into the continuing bull market. The sad fact is that the axiom of greed will take over and a large majority of the newcomers will want to stay in just a little bit longer for a little more gain and in a matter of days their investments will vanish.

Before getting into what the market will do in the coming years as we approach the peak of the financial markets and enter into the decline, let's take a closer look at the forces other than psychology that are driving this market in relation to long-wave theory.

We must remember that we are within an intermediate cycle that is advancing and complementing the effect of the long wave. This intermediate advance is naturally increasing the profit picture which creates an increase in earnings. There is an added increase to the profits and earnings picture by the existence of the long wave. A great deal of the improving profit picture is due to sagging and falling prices. This sounds unusual at first but when we take a closer look the reasons become evident. The falling prices first come in raw materials and commodities. For most industries this means their cost of production is lower. Of course falling prices are not good for the commodities industry as most of us are well aware that they have already entered the depression. What they are experiencing is an example of what is to come in the rest of the economy. The falling prices we are seeing in commodities are due to overexpansion and overcapitalization which creates oversupply. We all know that when the rest of the industrial world gets savings from the commodities and raw materials industries it is quite some time before those savings are passed on to the consumer.

The oil retail industry is a perfect and clear example. We have seen a drastic fall in oil prices but the consumer has yet to see gas drop the same percentage at the pump. This is happening in all areas of the economy. We have seen cost dropping, yet retail prices are holding their ground and even advancing in some cases. This naturally produces an increase in profits and earnings. As the quarterly reports are released, higher earnings drive up the price of stocks.

A slowing of inflation and dropping prices is perceived as an improving and stabilizing effect when taking an overall view of the economy. This positive perception helps bring buying strength into the market. Over the years there has been evidence to suggest that stocks can maintain a higher price-to-earnings ratio during a time of slowed inflation or deflation.

With earnings on the rise in coming years due to lower cost, coupled with the potential of higher PE's (price to earnings ratio) due to disinflation and potentially deflation, we will see enormous pressure for stocks to move upward.

Because of the overexpansion there is no need for mature companies to sink profits into new capital outlays. One only has to look as far as textiles, computers, autos, agriculture and other industries to see that the entire world is overproducing. There is expansion and development going on but this is by new and young companies whose management and owners perceive the good news in the economy that comes during the long-wave plateau as a time to enter the ball game.

This is an illusion brought on by the underlying forces at work in the economy. Most of these new companies go heavily into debt and will not survive the coming years. Since the established mature companies have excess capacity and have no need for more expansion and development, they naturally look to the stock markets which are on the move up for investment of their increased profits and excess capital. This is only fuel for the fire under the market and will help to push stocks even higher.

Over the past few years we have seen takeovers and stock buy-backs sweeping the marketplace. Maybe it is time someone take a close look at the reasons for this activity. The true reasons are simple while telling of the reckoning that is to come. If a company had excess capital and profits 10 or 20 years ago, they automatically went into new outlays and expansion of facilities. This was because the economy was still in its growing stage and every dollar was needed for investment to keep up with growing demand. Demand has fallen behind supply as we get into the peak of the long wave. This is why most industries are currently operating at well below capacity. Since companies are no longer needing to spend cash for expansion, we are beginning to see the largest corporate cash positions in history.

General Motors recently had a cash position of $9 billion. This cash was used to acquire EDS. As corporate cash positions begin growing during this time of slowed expansion and higher profits there is the natural tendency to start shopping around to see what can be bought. The sad situation is that these buyouts are causing companies to take on more and more debt when the smart move would be to use this cash to retire existing debt in order to tighten the belt in preparation for the bad times to come.

There has been a virtual explosion of acquisitions in the past couple of years. A few of these takeovers which are in negotiation, pending or already completed, are as follows: Beatrice, $5.1 billion; R.H. Macy, $3.6 billion; Continental Group, $2.8 billion; Storer Communications, $2.5 billion; Union Texas Petroleum Holdings, $1.7 billion; City Investing, $1.3 billion; Jack Eckerd, $1.2 billion; Northwest Industries, $1.2 billion; Metromedia, $1.1 billion; and Levi Strauss, $1.1 billion. The size and sort of these takeovers are unprecedented and prove to strengthen argument of the long wave's existence.

An amazing and telling figure is the enormous increase in the total amount of dollars spent on buyouts in recent years. The value of leveraged buyouts in 1981 was a mere $3 billion dollars. In 1982 this number was up a modest half billion to $3.5 billion. 1983 saw another increase to $4.5 billion while 1984 saw an explosion to $18.5 billion and the total for 1985 which only covered through the third quarter was an astounding $24.6 billion. And 1986 saw an amazing $200 billion in takeovers. Many would like to believe that these great increases are due to some sort of takeover fever and not to structural changes going on in the world economy.

I must say I wish they were right but economic decisions are based on concrete factors, not a passing biological condition. The fact is that the economy is overextended. The big money is not going into new layouts and production capacity but into the financial markets in the form of takeovers and acquisitions.

We discussed in Chapter Seven the effect the Fed is having on stocks by increasing the money supply. They are attempting to ignite inflation in an effort to prevent a deflationary collapse. But what we are seeing happen is that prices are staying down due to the great competition for markets in an overproducing economy and the new money the Fed is generating is pouring into the stock markets. The world is already awash with liquidity and the Fed is just adding to the problem. We should realize by now the only place for this liquidity to go is into stocks. This is only one more reason the stock markets of the world are moving up.

When is less more? When the number of outstanding shares on the market is shrinking while the number of dollars chasing those shares is increasing. All of these takeovers, as well as the stock repurchases by many companies who are seeing their own stocks as attractive investments, are rapidly diminishing the number of shares on the market. One estimate is that the number of outstanding shares on the big board fell by eight percent in 1985 alone. When supply is shrinking and demand is on the rise, the market has only one place to go — up.

The dollars spent by companies to repurchase their shares is only more fuel for the fire in the hands of the public as the axiom of greed runs its course. If there is any advice to companies from the long-wave reality, it is that instead of using their excess cash to buy other companies or buy their own shares they should be retiring as much of their expensive debt as possible.

The investor who is looking for a company that will survive the coming decline should look for a company that is lowering its debt to equity ratio and not being so cock sure of themselves as to buy their own shares on the open market. Of course there are few if any stocks, no matter how stable a position, that are going to move up as we enter the coming decline. The truly smart investor would get out of all stocks when the getting is good.

One element to the bull market that is often easily overlooked by economists is that as the market begins to move up in the plateau of the long wave it becomes a self-fulfilling prophecy that helps to drive it to new heights. Most companies maintain their own stock portfolios. During this time of rising stock prices these portfolios are adding to the profit and earnings of these companies. These improved earnings positions only give more steam and buying strength in the market by making these stocks more attractive. The stock market is not a zero sum game such as futures and options where I win and you lose. In a bull market I win and you don't win but you don't lose. This sort of no-lose predicament forces even more capital into the markets.

So what is the market going to do and when is it going to do it? First we will start with the current year 1987. We should see the Dow threaten or surpass 2,500 without a great deal of difficulty. The Kondratieff long-wave cycle is a fundamental approach to the economy and the financial markets and does not lend itself to technical analysis and short-term stock-market timing. You cannot look at long-wave theory and say that in this year on this day the stock market will peak and crash. Long-wave analysis can only say that we are in the plateau phase and headed for a stock market crash that will lead the world economy into a major depression.

At this printing, the market has collapsed as of Oct. 19, 1987 and it is probable that this is the long-awaited downturn in the financial markets. This crash has shattered market psychology and there is doubt that we will pull out of this incredible drop. It is my prayer we can pull out, so that there will be more time to prepare for depression. But I am afraid the damage has already been done and the world economy will soon come to a screeching halt.

Do not be fooled if the market does not fall immediately to lower levels. After the crash of 1929 the market held its ground for many months and a majority of investors thought we would pull out of the collapse. The market even had many large up days that brought hope into the minds of ardent bulls in the marketplace. As I have already said — if we do pull out of this crash and head higher for a season, the big crash will be far worse than Oct. 19, 1987. If this market gets over 3,000 in the next half-year, then the true crash, when it does come, may be over 1,000 points and a billion shares.

It would seem at this point that the underlying weaknesses have become apparent and the market has realized that the only economy underneath it is inflated expectations and expensive debt. All evidence points to the disturbing fact that another generation has ridden the crest of the long wave right over the edge.

The market should ultimately find its resting spot somewhere between 1992 and 1995 below 500 on the Dow Jones Industrial Average. Once again, the great pendulum will have ushered in the next era of purifying pain.

It is quite difficult to pinpoint the exact peak of the long wave in the stock market. Anyone who attempts to short this market or, on the other hand, hold out to the last minute, could be wiped out. Due to the undercurrents and volatility in the markets of the coming years, risky investment vehicles will take on added complexity. If you attempt to short this market and miss the turnaround by even a few weeks, you could be looking at a couple hundred points on the upside and thus be wiped out.

Any short positions should be taken after the market has taken a substantial drawback that smells of a collapse and that is clearly the long-awaited downturn of the long wave in the markets. There is no reason for the astute investor, who is willing to take a little risk and knows what to look for, not to make a windfall from the market conditions of the next few years and on into the decline. The amateur should play it safe and bet on the long-term guarantees of the Kondratieff long-wave cycle.

When considering stock market performance and market opportunities in the coming years, I am compelled to take a quick look at stock options and index options. With the sort of markets that will exist over the next few years the proficient options trader is presented with any number of possibilities for making a windfall in the markets. I discuss these potential investments with a great deal of caution.

Robert Prechter does an excellent job of outlining my reasons for caution: "I think it's going to be much more important to try to keep what you have than to try to make more. I probably won't advocate short-selling or put-buying to my subscribers and the reason is not a happy one. You may make money initially but before the crash is over many brokerage firms will be bankrupt or in danger of bankruptcy. You might have made tons of money on paper with your short sales and options but then you'll go to the window to collect and you won't be able to."

It should be clearly understood that the options markets possess enormous amounts of risk to the trader. It goes without saying that the other side of this coin is the exceptional profit possibilities for the one willing to assume the risk. I will not go into detail as to options trading and positions that should be taken but I will briefly outline the obvious. Straight buying in the options market is a gamble in any type of market and that includes a bull market. The mathematical odds are always clearly against the buyer. Although with the enormous upward momentum this market will posses over the next few years, it will be very tempting for the buyer of stock or index-call options to enter on any substantial weakness. The market will no doubt be very likely to come roaring back to hand the buyer three-digit percentage profits on numerous occasions.

The writer or seller on the other hand will be able to add to his already favorable odds the upward strength and momentum in the market — that is, as along as the bull market lasts. The writer should always cover his position.

A word of caution is that the writer should be in no hurry but should wait for the market to present him with a sufficient drawback of say five percent before he sells his position. This market will often offer such opportunities. Certain spreads and other creative positions will present the trader with excellent opportunities.

As we enter the coming decline in the markets and as we are pushed off the plateau of the long wave, there will be great opportunities in options by taking the opposite of the above-mentioned positions. In the coming years there is no doubt that the options markets will prove to retire quite a few traders who have the patience and stomach to play the averages effectively. Another word of caution is that one should find a broker who knows the options markets well and is forthcoming with his client on the risks and rewards involved. If your broker cannot communicate clearly the risk and rewards of options and make you completely understand the position you are taking then don't count on trading for long — your account balance will quickly vanish. Above all avoid the most common vice found in any market — greed.

Our observations of stocks have centered on the fundamentals of the long-wave cycle. In general I do not endorse technical analysis of the markets. This book has dealt exclusively with fundamental realities in the marketplace. There are two exceptions to my general write-off of technical analysis.

At this point it would be appropriate to mention briefly the work of Robert Prechter and Peter Eliades. It is my belief that

the technical work of these two men is a reflection of the fundamentals presented by Kondratieff. Their work fills the void left
by Kondratieff's work which does not allow for accurate timing
of price movements in stocks.

Prechter is editor of the newsletter *The Elliot Wave Theorist* and Eliades is the editor of *Stockmarket Cycles*. Both these
men have excellent records in market timing and would be far
better at picking the peak and timing for this market than myself.
They are long-term technicians whereas most technical analysts
cannot see beyond the end of their noses. I highly recommend
that any serious investor closely follow the work of these two
men—especially over the next few years. However, there should
be a warning here. The long wave is a sure bet to take its course
within a general framework just as the seasons come and go. Yet
the exact date and time of turning of the long wave in the markets cannot be pinpointed with the same precision.

It is very necessary that I spend some time discussing the
all-important factor of brokerage houses. It should be clear at this
point that there will be a great many companies that will not survive the coming collapse in the markets. It should also be clear
that the brokerage industry will be no exception. The worst con-
ceivable nightmare an investor could ever find himself in would
be to have his investments with a company that doesn't survive
the coming crash. There will no doubt be literally tens of thousands of investors who find themselves in this exact situation. If
you are caught, your investments could be tied up in litigation
for years if not lost forever.

Standard and Poors and numerous other companies publish
the financial information needed to make a quick check of a
brokerage company's financial condition. One source would be
the annual reports of the companies themselves. You will find
that many companies are already walking a thin line in terms of
financial stability. I will not take the liberty to expose the companies whose conditions are ripe for catastrophe although many
of the largest houses would be included. There are a few brokerage houses that have very strong financial positions and these are
the companies you should be invested with. Your financial con-
sultant should be aware of a few solid companies which would
be safe. Although the only stocks I would hold in the coming
crash would be gold stocks, there may be stocks an investor still
wants to hold no matter what he believes or knows is going to
happen. If the investor is going to own stocks during the coming
crash, whether gold stocks or other stocks for whatever reason,

he should not leave the stock certificates with his brokerage house no matter who he invests with. If you keep the stock certificates in your possession, you will be safe even if your broker is wiped out.

It would perhaps be appropriate to close with a quote from James L. Green, professor emeritus of economics at the University of Georgia. "Investors need to recognize that paper assets are nothing more than promises to pay. Paper assets are not equity. They are not something owned, but rather something owed."

14

Bonds

Of all market investments high-grade bonds are considered to be the safest. Bonds have lower yields since the bond investor assumes far less risk than does the stock investor. It is thought by many that bonds are immune from the effects of the business cycle but this is far from the truth. Kondratieff stressed the relationship between bonds and the flow of the long wave as he saw emerging from long-wave analysis a very distinct pattern for prices and yields on bonds. Kondratieff concentrated his study on government issues which are far more stable than corporate issues. He believed corporate bonds followed the same general pattern of government issues.

At this point in our study of the long wave it should be fairly easy to understand that the currents that drive the long-wave cycle would also push credit markets in a predictable direction. The predictable path of the credit markets is not conjured up for the sake of long-wave evidence but stands on its own as an independent witness to the long-wave flow of the economy. The relation of bond yields and prices to the Kondratieff Wave is a bit more difficult to understand than the other factors we have looked at but are nonetheless extremely important.

For long-term investment it is crucial to know the general pattern bonds follow. It would seem many brokers are only interested in maximizing their own return and do not have the best interest of their clients in mind. They ignore the undeniable long-wave evidence before them and the effect it has on bonds.

There is no doubt that fiscal and monetary policy both have an impact and leave their mark on the economic conditions of the day. But their effect is not as great as most economists would have us believe. They receive far more credit than they deserve as they scramble about to give the illusion that their impact is far more substantial than it indeed is. When we look closely we see they but cater to the forces at work as the economy takes its predictable long-wave path.

Short-term effects are all the credit we can legitimately give the budget and money supply manipulations of fiscal and monetary policy. It would perhaps be safe to say that the long wave doesn't react to policy but policy reacts to the long wave. These are important considerations in relation to the bond markets which owe their short-term activity to policy while they gain a long-term stamp from the rise and fall or the expansion and contraction of the long-wave cycle. This observation has proven to be critical information to the long-term bond investor.

Kondratieff's research showed a clear pattern for bond prices and yields emerging from his data. It became very clear that bond yields reached their lowest points during the low points or troughs of the long wave around 1848, 1896 and 1940. Yields began an upward movement in 1789 and peaked around the years just prior to the first downturn of the long wave. The downward pressure continued on yields and interest rates until we moved into the next upswing of the long wave in the mid-to late 1840s. This next rise in rates continued until the early 1870s as we prepared for the next economic decline of the long wave.

The evidence is clear that shows rates declining from their peaks in 1870 to the next trough of the long wave around 1896. From this time on we are more familiar with yields and rates. During this century we recall that yields and interest rates were slowly rising in the 1900s to their peak in 1922, from here they turned sharply down but then picked up slightly in 1928 and 1929, again to fall sharply until the early 40s. The comparison is all too clear as we saw rates rise once again from the early 40s to their peak in 1981. We have seen them fall off sharply during the 80s to their current levels.

From looking at the past it would perhaps be safe to predict that rates and yields should stay fairly steady or perhaps decrease a bit more in early 1987. They will begin to rise in 1987 until the collapse of the economy brings them down. Past declines have effectively brought rates down drastically. Demand for capital will vanish as the economy slides into deep depression. This will cause interest rates to collapse, except for junk debt, which will see rising rates until being purged from the system.

There is an inverse relationship to bond yields and the price of bonds which includes both government and industry. We have clearly seen price increases in bonds from around the peak in expansion to the end of the decline. Prices peak just before we enter the next long-wave expansion of the economy. The greatest bond rally in history was from the early 1920s until the early 1940s. There is no reason we shouldn't see a repeat on the same scale. We have witnessed this beginning in the early 80s and it should last until the mid- to late 90s. We will see a set back in the late 80s as rates pick up for a short time. This set back will be short lived as there will be a rush for the safety of the bond markets as the decline sets in. There have been and will be intermediate fluctuations of yields and prices. Long-wave theory concentrates on the overall trend in both yield and price where the existence of a long-wave pattern is all too obvious.

The role debt plays in understanding the long wave is very important and is closely related to the price performance and yields in the bond markets. Outstanding debt is lowest as we begin a long wave expansion in the economy and highest in the peak of the financial markets at the end of the plateau of the long wave. It is not important that "all" debt be flushed from the economy during the decline but that the debt which is unproductive and nonperforming be eliminated. This includes the outrageous debt of Third World nations, the enormous amount of debt taken on for leveraged buyouts, debt which has financed needless expansion and the mountain of debt that is choking the life out of the agricultural industry.

This debt is flushed out by the bankruptcies and failures during the decline. Individual, corporate and state debt are also at incredible levels and are beginning to show instability. There are many companies that kept their heads about themselves as the economy roared on over the past 25 years and did not expand beyond their means. These companies should do fine in the coming crash. They will have to cut back and streamline operations but will not be in danger of defaulting on their debt obligations. The sad fact is that most companies did not use prudent judgement in the past and will thus suffer for it in the near future. Debt is a useful instrument for business. We are all well aware that too much of a good thing can be deadly.

The coming economic decline and contraction will force companies which are inefficiently structured into default and bankruptcy. As we move deeper into the decline, more and more companies will be forced into submission. The banks which made the foolish mistake of loaning to companies beyond their means will be forced out of business. This will force and purge inefficiency out of the economy. Only the financially fittest of the business world will survive.

To understand the movement of the yields and prices of bonds in the long wave we must understand the supply and demand effect of capital (cash or money for investment) in relation to expansion and contraction. We have clearly seen that bond yields peak with interest rates as capital expansion peaks. This occurs as the economy enters the plateau as we saw in the early 20s and 80s. The decline in interest rates is a major factor in helping boost the stock markets to new highs.

We saw declines in rates in 1922 and 1981. These dates marked a turn in the world demand for capital to finance expansion. This has occurred leading into every plateau of the long wave. As in 1927 and as we will see again in 1987, an increase in demand for capital emerges for a short season at the end of the plateau before the crash. The euphoria in the markets coupled with rising earnings and profits will bring in new demand for capital which will soon be squelched by the crash of the stock markets and the deepening sharp decline. This increase in expansion is brief in new companies. The counterfeit entrepreneurs emerge on the scene during this period since it appears anyone can make a profit.

When the decline takes hold we see rates begin to slide again as the economy finally slides off the plateau and the house of cards created in the stock markets and banks come tumbling down. The demand for new capital virtually disappears in the crash and with it high bond yields and interest rates. The bonds which survive the initial crash, that have been issued by stable governments and prudent industries at fairly high rates, will turn in their best performance in years. We must realize that any company with competent enough management to maintain a strong position in such a volatile and reckless economy will be smart enough to call these high-yielding bonds in and issue new debt at the new low rates. Such a potential development should be taken into consideration when mapping strategy for the years ahead.

Another suggestion to the investor in bonds, just as was given the investor in stocks, is that he should demand to personally keep his bonds and not allow his brokerage house this privilege. The brokerage house that sells the investor his bonds may not be around after the crash.

The effect of supply and demand for capital becomes obvious as we enter the expansion. When the new expansion or next upswing in the world economy begins, there is once again a demand for capital. This naturally has an upward pressure on yields and there is no doubt that rates will continue to rise until the next peak of the long wave. Just as with any commodity, when the demand for money increases so does the price we pay for that money in the way of interest rates. We saw this as rates started to rise in 1789, 1846, 1896 and 1940. We will no doubt see it again in the mid- to late 1990s.

Another major consideration when planning bond strategy will be the psychological changes taking place as we enter a major world economic decline. Bonds have a safety factor since they take priority over stock, if the time ever comes for liquidation of the issuing firm. Bonds receive a safety premium over stock. As the decline sets in, the psychology of the marketplace will be changing from one of extreme optimism to one of extreme pessimism.

The demand for safety has great effect on the upward pressure on the price of bonds and has a downward pressure on yields. At the same time we see a great decrease in the demand for stock. There is growing strength in the minds of investors towards risk aversion as the new era of pain is ushered in.

The United States government has always been considered the safest investment in the world and government securities will have increasing prices brought on by the safety factor — I say this with caution. Rising prices should also be the case for the bond issues of stable foreign governments whose people will participate with citizens of the United States in the rush for security — this I also say with caution. This may startle many people but I believe that even though government bonds may offer great investments, I would place greater faith in AAA and AA corporate debt over United States bonds. I would recommend AAA and AA corporate investment over any public debt.

The one avenue of government investment that should prove to be safe and liquid is treasury bills. Treasury bills are the government's short-term borrowing instruments. The government must keep this market liquid otherwise Washington would have to shut down.

We have seen a major collapse in the stock market and a universal rush into the safety of bonds. If this is the beginning of a major depression, we will see a continued rally in the bond market from now until the late '90s. If we are given more time by a substantial rebound in the stock market, then we will have another short setback in bonds before the stock market crash that will bring a prolonged bond rally.

It should be pointed out that the rally in bonds that will come with a depression will only be in high-quality instruments. Low-grade and junk bonds will vaporize with the companies that issued them. A wise and prudent move would be to steer clear of any poorly rated bonds for the next ten years.

As we have discussed, there will be a rise in rates beginning in 1987 continuing until the crash. This will be pushing bond yields up and bringing a brief setback in the bond market by pushing bond prices down. Any investor who simply abhors risk and is going to stay clear of stocks should perhaps go ahead into the bond market realizing he may face a slight setback — that is if he plans to invest in bonds. He will be trading a slight drop in his bond prices for security during this dangerous time of the financial peak in the long wave.

I cannot emphasize enough that when looking at corporate bonds the only ones that should be considered would be highly rated and issues from stable, blue-chip companies.

In order to assist the investor, I thought I would provide a list of the only industrial and utility companies that remain AAA rated as listed by Standard and Poors:

Amoco	IBM Credit Corp.
Bristol-Myers	IBM
Campbell Soup	Illinois Bell
Carnation	Indiana Bell
Cincinnati Bell	Merck & Co.
Citizens Utilities	Minnesota Mining & Manufacturing
Chesapeake & Potomac Telephone of Virginia	
Diamond State Telephone	New Jersey Bell
Eli Lilly	Pfizer Inc.
Emerson Electric	Procter & Gamble
Exxon Corp.	Rochester Telephone
Exxon Pipeline	South Central Bell
Fort Howard Paper	Sterling Drug
General Electric	Wisconsin Bell

Other companies could be considered if they are closely analyzed and have secure market positions with extremely low debt-to-equity ratios. The investor should keep in mind when investing in bonds that most bonds are callable after five years by the issuer and you could be caught by having your bond called. Some bonds do not have this feature. One could wait until late in the 80s and purchase bonds that you could hold through the mid-90s before the possibility of having them called. By the mid-

90s it will be time to shift back into stocks and out of bonds. The investor who wants to truly maximize gains from his knowledge of the long wave would do well to stay in the stock market up to the end of the bull market before switching into bonds, gold or possibly some real estate. The catch is knowing when we are at the peak of the greatest bull market since the late 20s.

As I suggested in the last chapter, the peak in the stock market will also mark the low point in bond prices from the short slump they will be in because of rising interest rates for the short period before the crash. Most will not have any interest whatsoever in waiting until the last few days of the peak. A possible guideline would be to shift from stocks to bonds following the Fed's third increase in the discount rate. It is possible that the Fed will not have the opportunity to increase for the third time. It is really up to the individual investor on how far he will be willing to press his luck. The wise investor will have already completed his move into bonds, gold or small holdings in real estate. We will discuss real estate more fully in Chapter 16.

For risky investors there are excellent profits to be made in bond futures and interest-rate futures if one so desires. The late 80s should give those interested in going long in bond futures possibilities for profits available only during the beginning of the long-wave collapse. Those interested in interest rate futures should be short after three rises in the discount. Timing is again of utmost importance to the person attempting such positions and all elements to the long wave should be measured closely before making decisions. Such investment instruments are certainly not for the inexperienced investor.

In review of bonds we see that they do indeed follow, both in price and yield, the flow of the long-wave cycle. The investor should be aware of the long-wave effect on his bond holdings. He should be clear on the position he wants to find himself in during the coming years. The risk-averse as well as the risk-taker have a great deal to gain by observing the Kondratieff Wave in relation to bonds. The coming years are no time to be holding low-grade bonds that will be washed away along with the company that issued them. Many will ignore the evidence before them while making decisions in the bond market. Like the fisherman not interested in the flash-flooding upstream, many investors will be carried on the rising water to their ultimate ruin and downfall.

15

Gold

Gold has for thousands of years been the store of value in the world as well as being the chief measure of money. This is because of gold's many rare qualities. Only in 1971 was gold abandoned as a measure or backing of the United States dollar. Over the past few years we have seen gold reemerging as a form of payment in international transactions. This is going to have an enormous impact on gold and will greatly affect its value in the future.

There has been a great push in economic circles in recent years, on the part of the supply-siders to reinstate the gold standard in America. Inflation has not threatened revival and the economy has picked up steam thus the supply-siders' argument has lost its strength and it is very unlikely that such a standard will come about for the time being.

This is not to say a return to the gold standard would not be in the best interest of the United States. What I am saying is that due to the current perceived economic expansion it is very unlikely that we would move in that direction, at least for a number of years. Gold has been the heart of a great deal of speculation in the past decade and the world view of gold has undergone major changes.

Gold is a commodity but because of its unique and rare characteristics and indestructible qualities it will not follow price patterns of other commodities in the coming decline. Industrial uses for gold are increasing at a rapid pace. As one writer said: "Our age of high technology finds it indispensable in everything from pocket calculators to computers, telephones to television and missiles to spacecraft."

The amount of gold used in a single product has decreased due to price increases but its overall use has increased drastically. Gold is now being applied in industry with more caution and

153

far more efficiency. Where it used to be applied 20 microns thick on circuitry it is now applied only two microns thick.

The price fluctuations of gold in the past long-wave peaks do not really give us guidance for the projection of gold prices in the coming decline. In the past there was some link between the monetary system and gold, even if it wasn't a pure relationship. Gold was bought and sold by the government at set prices, so there could not very well be any increase or decrease in price.

Today there is no link at all and the dollar is a fiat money and not redeemable in any commodity. This is the case with the currencies of all other Western nations as well, except for the new European Currency Unit (ECU). The ECU is redeemable in gold.

During past declines there was always an increase in the demand for gold but because its price was not determined by the market there were no great price fluctuations. There were very severe shortages and hoarding of gold during these periods which in a free market, like we have today, would have driven the price up. Today the price of gold is determined by supply-demand conditions in the open market. This will drive the price up when the coming decline forces an increase in demand due to gold's perceived safety.

Before we look to the future and try to understand how gold will perform, let us first take an overview of the history of gold and what it is that makes it such an attractive and unique commodity. "What makes gold the noblest of metals?" asks one writer. "Its greatest strength is its indestructibility. Unlike silver, it does not tarnish and it is not corroded by acid-except by a mixture of nitric and hydrochloric acid. Gold coins have been recovered from sunken treasure ships after two centuries beneath the sea, looking bright as new ... Its beauty and versatility swiftly recommended it above all other metals. One ounce of gold can be beaten into a sheet covering nearly 100 square feet. It is also so ductile that one ounce can be drawn into 50 miles of thin gold wire. It is such an excellent conductor of electricity that a microscopic circuit of liquid gold 'printed' on a ceramic strip saves miles of wiring in a computer." It has been estimated that through all of history there has only been mined some 90,000 tons of gold. This may seem like an 'enormous amount but consider that, because of its density, this entire amount if melted down would measure less than 19 cubic yards which is less than three average size houses. This total world supply of gold if priced at $350 per ounce would come to just over one trillion dollars. A sobering thought in light of this fact is that all the gold in the world couldn't pay off half the United States' debt. The fact is that gold was in very short world supply before the middle of the 19th century and has only been available in large amounts for some 130 years.

Russia was producing some three-fifths of the world's output of gold in 1847 just prior to the discovery of gold in California. Mines near Mongolia on the Lena River east of Lake Baikal and on the Amur River discovered in the late 40s were producing over 40 tons in 1880 and over 60 tons in 1914. The "Age of Gold" was ushered in by California in the rush of 1848 to 1849. Until this time it is estimated that there had only been mined some 10,000 tons of gold in all of history.

It all began one afternoon in January of 1848 when James Marshall, a carpenter, found small specks of gold at John Sutter's mill at the junction of the American and Sacramento Rivers. The United States was in the process of completing the purchase of California and New Mexico from Mexico for $15 million in early 1848, just as the news of the gold find was spreading. By 1852 tens of thousands of fortune hunters and adventurers had flocked to California and had mined well over $81 million in gold in 1852 alone.

Australia was the nation next hit with gold fever when in 1850 there was a major gold find in New South Wales that yielded 26 tons in 1852 alone. Gold was discovered in a number of places in Australia but the world's largest finds were yet to come in South Africa where production reached 120 tons by 1898.

One last big strike before the end of the century came in the Klondike in 1896 as a couple of salmon fisherman saw a glimmer of gold on the bottom of a stream. The Klondike rush yielded over 75 tons of gold in the last three years of the 19th century, the biggest century for gold discovery in the history of man.

As gold poured into the money centers of Europe in the mid-19th century, there were dramatic effects on the world's economy and monetary systems. This was the time of the upswing of the second long-wave cycle and the gold discoveries did a great deal to boost the world economy and stimulate world trade. These great discoveries of gold paved the way for the introduction of the gold standard which became an international basis of money. A majority of currencies were attached to a fixed amount of gold from 1879 to 1913. Most of Europe abandoned the gold standard in 1913 and the United States finally followed suit during the banking crisis of 1931 after suffering a great drain on gold reserves to foreign nations, especially England.

On April 5, 1932, under the leadership of Franklin Roosevelt, it became illegal for United States citizens to hold or own any form of monetary gold, either coins or bullion. This should be a concern considering the inevitability of the coming banking crisis but should not pose too serious a threat since the government was doing this in 1932 in an effort to relinquish its responsibility to repay in gold. Today the government has no such obligations so it shouldn't find such blatant stealing from the American people to be necessary.

In order to get a feeling for the current nature of gold in the markets we must go back to the Bretton Woods agreement of 1944. The international banking collapse of 1932 left the world monetary system in shambles and countries unable to control and carry on fiscal policy without seeing their currencies depreciate in terms of gold, their capital flee the country or their credit markets crippled. This led to a meeting in Bretton Woods, New Hampshire and the creation of an international monetary agreement that would, because of its inherent contradictions, come crashing down 25 years later.

The basis of the agreement was that the dollar would be redeemable in gold but only by foreigners. United States citizens and banks were not allowed to exchange dollars for gold. The price of gold would be fixed at $35 to the ounce for the foreigners. The foreign currencies would be required to maintain fixed exchange rates with the dollar. They were allowed to rise and fall by only one percent from their fixed rates.

This had the effect of treating the dollar as gold, at least in relation to foreigners. The United States Federal Reserve had the treasury print more and more money. Naturally the dollar became extremely overvalued against foreign currencies. Foreign governments were forced to print large amounts of their own currencies in order to buy the excess of dollars. The dollar was overvalued by all measures. Being convertible into gold, the dollar was being traded in for gold almost as fast as it was being printed. Foreign governments would much rather have gold locked away in their vaults than the overvalued dollar. The dollar was convertible by both foreign commercial banks and the central banks of foreign nations. Converted it was as the United States' gold reserves peaked at 701 million ounces in 1949 plummeted to 296 million ounces in 1968. The United States Air Force was making constant flights of cargo planes loaded with gold from Fort Knox to London during this period.

Because of the significant devaluation of the dollar, as the presses rolled on during the Bretton Woods agreement there began an upward pressure on the market price of gold sometime in the early 60s. In order to stop this upward pressure the central banks had begun open-market efforts to hold the dollar up and hold gold down. These open market efforts were mainly composed of the United States selling large quantities of gold in an effort to keep the price of gold down.

At the realization that gold could not be held down indefinitely there was a meeting called in Washington in 1968 during which a "two tier" market was established where central banks would continue to operate in gold at the official level of $35 per ounce and the free market would be allowed to find its own price.

Central banks were forbidden to participate in the open market. This of course did not stop the erosion of the dollar. All European currencies were coming closer to pushing through their limits set in the 1944 agreements. This was clearly due to the fact that the gold dollar was losing its shine.

England was the first to violate the agreements and devalue its currency. All of Europe soon followed suit. This caused a massive flight into gold but the United States still honored its gold dollar at $35 per ounce. In 1971 United States gold reserves were getting extremely low and were pushing below their 25-percent backing of reserve notes.

Rumors began to spread that the United States was going to close the gold window. No longer would gold be exchangeable for the dollar.

This would cut the dollar loose from any backing and allow the devaluation of the dollar to go unchecked. This rumor caused a new-style gold rush and in one week some $4 billion in gold left the country.

On Sunday, August 15, 1971, rumor became reality as President Nixon in a televised address announced the closing of the gold window and that no more gold would be given in exchange for United States dollars. The only market that now existed for gold was the free market and gold prices took off with a vengeance. When the gold dust had settled, United States gold reserves had fallen from over 22,000 tons to under 8,300 tons while European gold reserves had exploded to over 17,000 tons.

We have seen gold prices soar from a low of $34.75 in 1971 to their high of $850 per ounce in 1980. Gold has since dropped to the $300-per-ounce range then rebounded to over $400 per ounce at the present time.

One of our main objectives in long-wave analysis is to determine what effect it will have on investment instruments. The question of the moment is: "What is the price of gold going to do?"

In the mid- to late 70s there were many financial advisors running around saying to buy gold at any price; the sky was the limit. Indeed the sky was the limit, at which point gold abruptly plummeted. This advice cost clients dearly and I am afraid could continue to cost them into the late 80s.

There are a number of wonderful ideas on gold; many attach gold to a strict inverse relationship to the dollar. There are good reasons for this assumed relationship but many put far too much faith in gold performing the opposite of the dollar. This is what I call the "window on the fingers syndrome," created when Nixon slammed the gold window on quite a few fingers. The fact is that as you enter the peak of the long wave, tendencies in financial markets are quickly broken and we have seen the gold-dollar inversion law broken on a number of occasions.

I am sorry to inform these inversion die-hards that gold is now an investment considered to be a safe haven. Of course, the collapse of the dollar would be extremely bullish for gold as it would take the place of the dollar as the world's medium of exchange. In the long run, gold could surpass United States savings bonds in safety consideration and thus react to international economic conditions accordingly.

On a number of occasions over the past few years we have seen gold move up in reaction to negative economic news and move down in reaction to positive economic news. We will see this very clearly in the coming crash.

A major factor to consider when looking at gold is the impending collapse of the international monetary system. We have seen this in every decline of the long-wave cycle. We are well aware that this has always led to major changes in the system. There is reason to believe that gold will play a major role in the coming changes to the monetary system which could make it an extremely attractive investment to be in when the collapse occurs. Anyone who truly understands the forces at work in the monetary system today agree that this collapse is only a matter of time away.

Taking all things into consideration we should see gold in the $350- to $550-dollar-an-ounce range over the next few years. Anywhere in this price range gold is a reasonable buy.

The wise investor will wait until attractive purchasing opportunities present themselves in the next few years and should not rush in just for the sake of buying gold. The market will present the buyer with a number of opportunities for buying gold at a good price. The year 1988 should prove to be an excellent time to purchase gold. The price of gold should explode as we slide into the coming decline and collapse. Gold will be perceived as the safest haven and store of value.

As this new demand for gold comes in, the price could easily exceed $1,000 an ounce in a matter of months — especially as rumors of a new gold standard surface. Even if the price of gold does not explode upward, its purchasing power will rapidly increase as other values collapse, which would still make gold an excellent investment. Gold will always be accepted as a form of payment.

Kondratieff related the buying power of gold and the production level of gold very closely to the long-wave cycle. Since production prices reach their peaks as the long-wave expansion peaks, it becomes extremely expensive to mine gold. At the same time the purchasing power of gold is declining. This tends to slow production as we enter the peak of the industrial expansion of the long-wave cycle.

The opposite occurs in the decline with production prices falling and the purchasing power of gold increasing. As the decline deepens, the cost of labor and the price paid for mining equipment gets cheaper while the purchasing power of gold is on the rise. This naturally leads to greater production efforts and output as the long wave reaches its low point in the trough of the decline. The confusion in the markets and the crash of the banking system will create a rush for the safety of gold. The free markets we have today will put great upward pressure on the price of gold during the coming decline.

Throughout history those who have held gold have always come out on top when times are bad. The buying power of gold has consistently gained while all else has fallen by the wayside. Paper money supported by nothing can only last for a season and — like everything else that has no foundation — it will soon be washed away. Gold will have a double advantage in the coming decline. It will increase in purchasing power as deflation sets in and will be the basis to the world's new currency.

It would be wise to hold a significant amount of gold coin in one's readily available possession as the coming decline could be more severe than anyone could anticipate.

Clearly this was the case with the Great Depression. Only you could be the judge of the amount of gold this should be. All gold holdings should be in ingots or widely circulated coin. The Canadian maple leaf would be a perfect coin to hold because of its purity and acceptability. The maple leaf comes in one-ounce, half-ounce, quarter-ounce and 1/10-ounce coins. An IRA can be invested in United States coins which is a consideration for many investors. All gold other than what one keeps in his immediate possession should be stored in safety deposit with an institution the investor knows well. Of course extremely large holdings would be held in bullion bars and should only be purchased and held through well-established firms with excellent long-standing reputations.

Gold stock mutual funds may be an attractive form of investment in gold for the small as well as the large investor. This should be closely considered. It may be smart to divide your gold investments between gold stocks or gold mutual funds and actual gold holdings. One-half in stocks and one-half in coin, ingots or bullion bars would perhaps be the best mix. This all depends on the amount of your investments you plan to put in gold and your personal preference. The tendency for gold stocks to move up more on a percentage basis than gold itself should be kept in mind. Gold stocks may perform better than the actual price of gold in the coming years.

There is always the fearful possibility that the government may once again seize private gold holdings as in 1932. We certainly hope this would never occur. Although this should be a warning in case extra precaution is desired. Sufficient steps should be taken to protect oneself against such a possibility. This clearly presents the advantages of holding gold funds or stocks.

In review of this chapter we see that the long wave suggests gold as an important part of monetary policy of the past and future. It would indeed be a good idea to include it in your personal plans and objectives for the coming years as a potentially profitable position in your portfolio. History has proven that gold has survived what nothing else can and that only gold "is as good as gold."

16

Real Estate

The reality that the value of a home can go down just as easily as it goes up cast a revealing light on the idea of an economic long wave passing through the capitalist economy every 50 years. A major concern for the average homeowner and the investor alike is the effect the Kondratieff long wave has on the value and price of real estate.

When referring to real estate we are including not only residential but commercial and industrial property. The erosion of world prices that we have seen during every long-wave decline has also been seen clearly in the value of real estate. This is of utmost concern to the homeowner who has taken on enormous debt over the past 20 years of the upswing of the long wave. Many homeowners will soon be faced with large monthly payments on an asset that will be rapidly decreasing in value. Home values have already begun their descent in many areas. Over the past few years we have seen the erosion of home prices for the first time since the Great Depression.

For the first time in 50 years we are seeing that in many cases families are finding it cheaper to turn the house over to the bank than make the payments they can't afford. A majority of these instances are occurring in the heartland of America in the energy and agricultural regions.

Deflation in residential real estate will occur across the board as the coming decline sets in.

For years if a family came on hard times and came up short on payments they could sell their house for a small gain without much effort. Things have changed. In increasing numbers families are running into difficulty selling their homes. Whether due to hard times or just because of a necessary move, many families are finding that their homes will not sell on the open market for what they have in them. Under such circumstances many are finding it is a wise move to simply allow the bank to

161

foreclose and take the home. This exact scenario has occurred thousands of times in the past few years and is occurring with increasing frequency with every passing day. Although the worst-hit areas have been concentrated in the central United States in recent years, the problems in the heartland are going to spread quickly to both coasts in the near future.

The changes that are occurring today mark the need for tremendous strategy changes on the part of families and businesses involved in real properties. This is of course a majority of the families in America and most businesses in operation today.

The following quote from a *Wall Street Journal* September 4, 1986, article gives piercing insight into the many problems facing real estate investors: "Tomorrow looks bleak to hundreds of developers, lenders and investors, the victims of a deflation in commercial real estate that began sporadically in the early 1980s but in the past year has deepened and spread geographically. In many cities, office rents that support the prices of skyscrapers have dropped 25 percent to 40 percent. Occupancy rates at certain kinds of hotels, apartments, resort properties and condominium high-rises have also plummeted and in most cases so has their value. Cities once thought immune to a real estate recession, such as San Francisco, Salt Lake City, Phoenix, Chicago and Dallas, are being hammered. In areas already hurt by the energy slump, such as Houston, Denver and Tulsa, things have grown markedly worse."

Many who use real estate as a tax shelter and as a hedge against inflation will soon find that the game is being played on an ever-tilting playing surface. This calls for their positions to be closely analyzed and restructured in the coming years. *The Wall Street Journal* article pointed out that vacancy rates in commercial real estate are reaching unheard-of proportions.

In many cities development has come to a screeching halt. Many are not willing to accept the fact that the true cause of what is going on today in the real estate industry is due to major shifts in the structure of the economy brought on by the plateau of the long wave that we currently find ourselves in.

Many who were once skeptical of the facts are beginning to change their tune as they observe the real estate evidence which is overpoweringly in favor of the long-wave hypothesis.

To gain direction for what position one should be taking during the coming years we must first take a close look at the causes and conditions in the economy that have created the situation in which we now find ourselves.

As the economy initially moves into the expansion of the long-wave cycle, inflation is just beginning to show its face. Prices, including real estate, which have taken a beating for some time, begin moving in an upward direction brought about by an increase in demand across the board. As the new upswing begins, interest rates begin to pick up from the lows they reached in the trough of the long-wave cycle. These factors all have the effect of moving real estate prices in a steady upward direction throughout the entire long-wave upswing of the economy. Inflationary pressures are increasing as the economy moves further into the expansion making real estate extremely attractive as a hedge against inflation. The further we move into the expansion the easier it is to forget that prices will eventually come down. Such has been the case for investors in real estate today who are under the illusion that prices can only go up. We know that inflation subsides in the peak of the upswing. We saw this in the early 20s and early 80s when there was no longer the rush into real estate as during the extremely inflationary period through which the economy had just passed.

This is important to the investor for two reasons: 1) it erodes demand for real estate, exerting downward pressure on real estate prices; 2) it frees up more money for the stock markets that are always reaching new highs during this period.

We only have to look as far as the average family farm in America to see the long wave taking its effect on real estate. Farmland prices have been plummeting in recent years and there is no sign that a firming of prices is on the horizon. In many areas land prices have fallen by as much as 50 percent.

The effect this is having on the agricultural industry is all too obvious as we have seen failure after failure in all parts of the country. This situation was created by oversupply and overexpansion as we thoroughly discussed earlier. What has happened on the farm is an excellent example of what is in store for the rest of the real estate market. As the economy slows dramatically in the coming years of decline, the demand for real estate will virtually disappear. This will bring prices down substantially from their current levels.

Those who believe the plight of the farmer to be an isolated predicament need only look as far as the local neighborhood to see housing prices sliding lower for the first time since the early to mid-1920s. Prices should firm a bit in the late 80s as they did in the late 20s but will then plummet as the economy slides off its plateau into the decline. The overexpansion and capitalization in real estate, just as in the agricultural industry, eventually forces a slowing and then turning of prices from constantly rising to gradually eroding until they drop dramatically as they did in 1819, 1873 and 1929.

It would be easy to come to the conclusion that this is no time to be investing in real estate. It is true that real estate should not be bought or held in the expectation and anticipation of resale in a few years for a capital return. This is not to say do not invest in real estate at all for the coming hard times. Actually I highly recommend investment in real estate. My advice to invest in real estate is not in order to realize a profit but to realize a factor of safety that no other investment can give.

There are of course a number of considerations to be made when evaluating the position one would want to hold in the coming years in relation to real estate. These considerations cover everything from the wealth of the investor to the amount of risk the investor is willing to assume. Whatever the situation, real estate will play a major role for everyone in the coming years as everyone must live somewhere even if Central Park.

There is no investment which has the safety value of real property or real estate. This covers land, houses, apartments, castles and anything else that finds itself in a permanent place. Investment in real property protects the investor from what I consider to be the long-wave unpredictables. There are any number of complications that can arise during a severe economic downturn that will affect all investment instruments with the exception of real estate.

Stocks, besides decreasing rapidly in value due to overall economic conditions or individual corporate failures, are subject to complexities in transactions and in the brokerage end of transfer of ownership. If you were flawless in your market picks and your overall timing, your broker could still make a mistake that could cost you dearly. Many will find that their brokerage firms themselves are in financial trouble and are forced into bankruptcy because of their own foolish market transactions. So even without making a wrong move yourself you may find your investment washed away by another's mistakes or you may find your assets frozen for years while litigation drags on and you are left helpless.

You may find your banking deposits frozen during the restructuring of the banking system. This sort of thing will never happen with the ownership of real estate. As long as the title was thoroughly searched by an experienced, dependable lawyer you will not run into the predicament of suffering for someone else's mistake. Real estate is something you can jump up and down on, saw a tree down on, see with your own eyes and walk on with your own two feet.

There are numerous long-wave unpredictables which real estate protects the investor from. The danger in bonds is the fact that they can be called and again the broker or company making your transaction is always subject to error especially in the volatile markets we are going to see in the coming years.

When safety is a consideration, real estate reigns supreme. This would bring us to the conclusion that the investor should be concerned with far more than profit during the coming decline. He must realize that even though real estate will not bring a profit in the coming years, it possesses a quality no other investment has. That quality is real estate's true permanence.

Residential income properties should make excellent investments in the years ahead. Apartment buildings provide wonderful opportunities if buying is done carefully. People will always need a place to live. One would not want to hold any debt on such an investment except in very special circumstances. Rents can always be cut in a deflating economy and still provide the investor with sufficient income.

While we are considering the safety of real estate it would perhaps be appropriate to offer a word of caution when forming real estate partnerships during this period of intense long-wave activity. Many people have come to realize the hard way that partnerships in real estate can lead to conflict beyond one's wildest dreams. If you must have a partner you should be well aware of his financial position and condition. You would not want to see your safety hedge overridden by the mistake of having a partner without the insight you yourself possess. Complications could come as well from factors your partner has no control over but would still affect you adversely.

I would highly recommend independence in any safety hedge in real estate during the coming years. Hard times can destroy a relationship faster than anything to date. There is no reason to put yourself in that position.

Another word of warning to the investor in real estate comes under the topic of debt. The first and foremost investment of anyone during this time would be to have your principle location of residence debt-free with no liens or claims outstanding from any source. This is tall order for most individuals as I am well aware.

The most serious drawback to the new tax laws is that due to the elimination of the interest deduction most homeowners are shifting their consumer debt onto their home equity. When the coming decline gets under way many a homeless family is going to wish they had never heard of the home-equity loan. One of the smartest moves any family could make at this time is to get their home totally debt-free. There will be no excuse for any individual to stay in the market too long thus missing the opportunity to pay off his mortgage. This will prove to be a grave mistake.

The first responsibility of any investor is to provide a home for his family as the coming years will be a difficult enough time without losing your home. If the entire amount cannot be paid off it should at least be paid down to a manageable level so that after the coming fall in prices you would still have sufficient equity in your home. This would be in the neighborhood of 40 percent of the current market price of your home or less. Of course you will need an excellent source of income to meet even that obligation in the future. It would be recommended that if at all possible the entire home should be debt free as those long-wave unpredictables could come into the picture, including the loss of job security.

In some cases where home debt cannot be paid off it would be advisable for the homeowner to sell before the coming collapse in order to receive a good price on his home and realize the equity he has accumulated. This would be a difficult decision and should be considered carefully, measuring all the pros and cons. There were many people in mid-1929 who could have come out of the market and paid off their home mortgage several times over yet lost their homes after the crash. This should be a warning to many for the coming years.

I find myself humored by the nothing-down, get-rich-quick schemes in real estate that claim to guarantee success by taking on debt in the anticipation of rising prices. These plans which have made quite a few paper millionaires during the days of hyper-inflation and rising prices will prove to be close to the top in the list of casualties during the coming decline.

These get-rich-quick schemers will get just what they deserve in proportion to their work—"nothing." Debt could be useful in the coming years but it will be a delicate position that can produce the exact hedge necessary to gain in the coming decline. If the investor is of sufficient means there is no reason that he could not effectively use debt in certain real property positions to actually gain from the decline in prices. Many will be in positions to deal with banks to renegotiate debt by having the power to pay that debt off if necessary. A strong financial position could actually prove to make real estate profitable in the decline but this is not for the small investor. The no-money-down man best be shopping for large cardboard boxes in which to house his family as the bankers get their revenge on such low-life.

Real estate that has no debt obligations could be used to secure funds for other investments as we begin the next long-wave expansion in the late 1990s and should be considered by the investor in that light. He could gain far more by using other investments in the coming years but nothing could grant him the security that he would have in owning real property. Real property is an excellent avenue to take for the extremely risk-averse individual.

It should be noted that certain areas of the United States and the world, for that matter, are not nearly as inflated as others in property prices and could hold up quite well in the coming years of economic decline. Areas that will be hit the hardest are resort locations and other properties that do well in times of general prosperity. Well established and historical neighborhoods should suffer the least.

Tax considerations could prove to be major in real estate investment in coming years. Many people will no doubt be making large profits off the current and future bull markets. These profits will be taxed heavily unless a loss is shown. A safe position in real estate could be written off after its sale, thus used to offset the large gains in the stock and bond markets while providing a degree of security. The decision could always be made to hold onto the real property and pay the taxes.

Looking at real property in this light becomes more complicated but should be looked into closely by the astute investor. A consideration for the smaller investor is that since all prices will be adjusted downward, there is a good chance that we will see a substantial drop in taxes on real property as we move into the decline due to the falling value of the property. This could be important to many who look closely at inflows and outflows in an effort to balance their future finances.

Overall the tax advantages in holding real estate, coupled with its safety, could be exactly what many investors are looking for to maximize their returns while maintaining a sense of security in the coming years.

Another area of possibility when looking at real property for investment in the coming years is property futures contracts for the the high-risk investor or the investor who wants to hedge his position. Futures contracts are becoming more and more common in real properties, tying the participants to certain price commitments which during a time of volatile movements in real property prices could be used very successfully to maximize one's position using the predictable path of the Kondratieff long wave.

If one desired to do so, he could hold a real estate position and sell the right to someone to buy that position in the future, say three years out. The person who bought the future agreement would pay a premium which the seller would pocket as profit because the land will actually go down in value and the buyer will forfeit his right to buy it as he sees its value diminish.

You could also make a good profit by taking short positions in the coming years, forcing someone to buy land from you at high prices. These instruments could be used to cover your losses as prices decline on the property you own while giving you a secure position by holding real property. There will always be someone who believes land prices are still going up. These contracts are again only for the investor who enjoys a high degree of risk and is willing to face the consequences of his maneuvers, for better or worse.

In looking ahead we should see real estate emerging as an excellent buy-and-hold investment as we get into the mid- to late 1990s. By that time, the next expansion of the long wave should just be getting under way and prices will once again be on the rise.

In review we must emphasize that there is no investment with the physical security of real estate. It must be realized that the coming years of the late 80s and early 90s will be no time for a buy-and-hold position if one is looking for profits.

Real estate will have tax advantages that could be utilized quite effectively if done with careful planning and caution and could conceivably be used to hedge profitably in the coming years. Above all, real estate provides a roof over your family and this should not be jeopardized for any amount of profit.

17

The Crash: A Scenario

We have taken a close look at the history of the long-wave cycle as well as its effect on many different areas of life. In the last section we looked at basic investment instruments and how they should perform over the next few years as we reach the long-wave peak in the financial markets.

Part IV:

Looking to the Future

It would perhaps be beneficial for us now to take an overall view of the long wave and interweave all the material we have covered in an effort to better understand what the coming years have in store.

This chapter is an attempt to project, if only through speculation, what the next few years will be like. We will discuss what signs we should look for as we approach the edge of the plateau of the long wave and enter a period of economic contraction and decline.

The most dangerous occupation in the world is that of a prophet and I certainly do not claim to be one. I am not under the illusion that I can see the future but simply that through study of the long-wave cycle I understand the underlying forces at work and the direction these forces are pulling the economy.

Many are confused with the different signals coming from the economy today. Taking an overall view of the long wave and its enormous impact on the whole of life the seeming contradicting signals are beginning to make sense and come into focus as the observer becomes aware of their total relation to the long wave. At first glance it would seem a contradiction that we could be reaching new highs in the markets while internationally the debt crisis is reaching astronomical proportions. Many are frustrated with seeing world commodity prices falling drastically and for the first time in decades, pushing us into a period of real price deflation. It is equally difficult to understand the conservative politics of the day while socially we are becoming more liberal. Let us now take the evidence and data available and chart a path the world may indeed follow for the next few years.

The last years of this decade will see the world watching in amazement the heights the stock markets will attain. This will not be limited to New York but will also be the case in Tokyo and London not to mention the other exchanges such as the NASDAQ market and other smaller international markets. Many will say these heights are not to be feared because they don't possess the inherent flaws of the system of the 20s, such as no margin requirements and too few regulations.

This argument has little value. Now, instead of the investor having to buy on credit, the market is flooded with liquidity because of less-than-responsible monetary and fiscal policy on the part of all capitalist nations.

The difference between a 50-percent margin requirement and a 10 percent requirement will scarcely be noticeable, but still the market stability will be defended. The great paper profits being made in the markets will give the economy the illusion of having far more strength than it truly has and no real worries or changes will come from those capable of making a difference.

The view of a booming economy and its strength will be attributed to the current administration's policy of deregulation. The Reagan administration deserves praise for many of the steps taken to deregulate. But there is a danger in this. Deregulation is good for the economy at particular times. Too much deregulation when the economy is on a knife edge of instability, as we have in the peak of the long wave, can be extremely dangerous. There is no doubt we will see an increase in deregulation of every industry in the last years of this decade. This presents a frightening predicament since there will be little belief that the economy really is in a precarious position.

Forces unleashed by deregulation can and will contribute to the coming decline and make it far more painful than it has to be. We are already beginning to see what can happen when the deregulators become over zealous in their efforts. Damage can already clearly be seen due to the deregulation of the banking and securities industries. Recent deregulation allows banks into the brokerage and discount brokerage business. These new players are encouraging and forcing more money into the stock markets that are already over supplied with cash.

The deregulation in interstate banking will cover up the true problems in many of our banks by allowing troubled banks to be swallowed by others who themselves have no business making the acquisition. We are seeing this happen in many areas that are in trouble from energy and agriculture loans. This form of deregulation will only stall the coming day of reckoning.

The deregulation of any industry will force increased competition thus driving prices lower. Lower prices are certainly not inherently evil. A majority of the time falling prices would be a welcome sight but deflation is the final force that drives the economy to its knees in relation to the long-wave cycle. I wholeheartedly support the free market and increased competition.

What many do not realize is that since this helps to overexpand the economy it eventually helps bring about the long-wave decline. We need to have deregulation and hands-off policies from government as we are just beginning the expansion of the long wave and not just when entering the plateau.

As we move into the decline, people attribute the economic contraction to deregulation which does not deserve the blame. By eventually encouraging the decline, deregulation helps in its own demise because an economy in shambles brings about more regulation. This presents us with a Catch 22 situation for deregulation.

The past few years we have heard the battle cry of, "Power to the people," as there has been a great push to get the government off our backs. This will no doubt play a role on the political scene in the coming years as we hear this philosophy growing ever stronger. The late 80s will see further political lobbying for deregulation as the *laissez faire* attitude intensifies.

As soon as we find ourselves sliding into the next decline you can bet your bottom dollar that there will be pleading across every front for government assistance and once again regulation instead of deregulation will be the winner. This is all part of the swing of the pain and pleasure pendulum.

A small child gives us an excellent example of this as he seeks freedom from his mother who reluctantly grants it. But as soon as he gets out of control running downhill and trips and scratches his knee he comes rushing back to the safety of mother's arms or Uncle Sam's — as the case may be.

The U.S. economy has deregulated its way out of Uncle

Sam's arms and is currently preparing for a fall that will invariably bring it back to Uncle's perceived safety. Deregulation will be a popular rallying point in the coming years as it is today but, as it is seen as a cause of the economic hard times to come in the early 90s, the concept of deregulation will become very unpopular. It should be remembered that deregulation is only one element that will play a vital role in the coming crash.

Political conservatism will continue to be a powerful force in the late 80s. We discussed in Chapter Five as well as briefly in Chapter 11 that we find an unusual inversion taking place in the plateau of the long wave. This is that we tend to be very conservative politically and economically while our personal lifestyles and social behavior becomes far more liberal. The notion that the individual has perfect control over his destiny, brought on by a carefree, painless life of pleasure, promotes and encourages loose social and moral values. These carefree views are shattered by the pain of an economic decline.

This would lead us to the realization of a tendency towards a more immoral world over the next few years in terms of Judeo-Christian values. Increasing divorce rates and teenage pregnancy coupled with a general deterioration of value systems will be common over the next few years of the late 80s. We will then change to a more moral and socially conservative world as the decline begins and deepens.

As the decline sets in, conservative politics will soon be forgotten while conservative lifestyles will gain sweeping acceptance. If you look closely at the conservative politics of today you see that they stop at politics and economics and do not enter the lifestyle of the individual. When we enter the decline it is very likely that conservatism will enter into lifestyles as it is scourged from politics and economics. There is the great potential for religious revival across the world as people look to a force beyond themselves in times of economic depression.

There were great religious revivals sweeping the world during the Great Depression and there is no reason to think that the coming decline will prove to be any different. As the decline sets in, people will realize they need far more than pride and pleasure to survive the hard times.

The religious right that is caught up in politics today may well find itself overcome by a great swing into liberal politics and will be forced back to its original task of religious revival. People will turn towards religion in growing numbers and seek help from the government in their time of crisis.

Forces could emerge that would keep conservatism and the religious right in politics as we enter the decline. The conservative right would tend to help us pull out of the coming decline far more effectively and with longer lasting results than could liberal party politics. We must remember that the conservative right gaining reelection in 1992, as the decline and crash is under way, is highly unlikely but still possible.

The corporation will be caught in the same general trap of the carefree individual. It will assume that the surge in activity and declining prices will be good for the economy and that we are entering a new era of permanent prosperity where there is no such thing as the business cycle. Corporations will be tempted to join in the excitement of the markets.

In the next few years we will see an ever-increasing number of takeovers and buybacks. A few companies will realize the shallowness of the excitement and will be prepared for the slow-down when it comes. The companies with this vision will be few and far between. The general atmosphere during the coming years before the crash will be optimistic and positive as even corporate leadership will begin to believe the economy can move perpetually upward. It will be a difficult decision for companies to bring down debt instead of getting involved in the markets.

Earnings and profits will be steadily improving as we move into the late 80s and there will be room for celebration but not to the degree that it will be carried in the stock markets. Corporate performance will appear excellent in the late 80s and in many ways a major downturn will seem impossible. All things considered the years leading us up to the decline should be a time of positive reports and exceptional performance.

It is the underlying forces that give cause for extreme concern, such as large debts and falling prices coupled with increased protectionism, not to mention overexpansion and oversupply. Falling prices are very beneficial for a time but the destructive effects of deflation will soon begin to show up as expensive debt becomes more difficult to handle. The underlying contradictions for a strong economy will soon begin to erode confidence and stability in the marketplace.

Protectionism must be addressed in relation to the next few years and the coming decline. The further we get into the current recovery, the more pressure we are feeling for protectionism. This is not restricted to the United States but is a major issue facing virtually every trading nation in the world.

The trend towards protectionism is a sure mark of a long-wave peak because of the pressure brought on by overexpansion which naturally, in a free and open market, forces prices down because of over supply.

We are hearing cries for protectionism in an effort to protect markets that are being flooded with goods from industries that are overproducing. The trend will only intensify as we move into the close of this decade and there is downward pressure on international prices.

Rationality always seems to play second fiddle to politics. Many politicians will push for protection simply on reelection considerations, always knowing that in the long-run their constituents will suffer for their action. These politically based decisions will only make the coming trade decline deeper and more severe than it has to be. Protectionism will actually hurt the economy and should be done away with entirely if the coming decline is to be shortened.

It was runaway protectionism, such as the Smoot-Hawley Act, that caused a major portion of the damage done in the 1930s. Protectionism will be on the rise and there is no doubt that a great deal of protectionist legislation will be passed by many countries. This will only serve as insurance that we will indeed have a major economic downturn.

The Federal Reserve Board will play a role in the coming years in so much as they react to the Kondratieff wave. Many would argue with the position that the Fed does not set rates but that they accommodate the market. Sure they can manipulate for the short term, but in the long run, rates are going to do what the market demands. We have seen the Federal Reserve Board ease somewhat to accommodate for the unsuspected drop in inflation.

As prices firm in the late 80s, just as we saw in the late 20s due to the forces that give the illusion of an economy that is picking up steam, we will see the Fed tighten to try and slow things down. Rates will begin to rise slightly late in the decade. But as the economy comes crashing down with the markets the Fed will have no choice but to slash rates in the early 90s as we begin the long-wave cycle all over again.

The international political arena should be fairly placid over the next few years in terms of armed conflict. In the past long-wave plateaus and declines, there have been no conflicts among major powers. We will see the usual regional skirmishes but no major conflict should break out until we get into the next long-wave expansion. When nations are in internal economic turmoil, such as lies just over the horizon, it is usually no time to go stomping off over borders in search of conquest.

Slowly but surely the last surge in the long wave will come to a close in the stock markets. The effort to stimulate a dying world economy will find no success. More and more people will begin to recognize the signs of a dangerous situation which could easily send the world into another depression. By this time there will be nothing that can be done.

The panic button will not yet be pushed while the wise and perceptive investor begins to secure his position by getting out of the stock markets and into stable and safe investments. The name Kondratieff will begin to be heard whispered in board rooms and planning sessions and the fear of his prophecy once again coming to fruition will send terror through the minds of those who understand the true gravity of the situation at hand.

It is indeed a hard thing to fathom that another age of prosperity for the capitalist system will have come to an end.

Up to this point it doesn't sound as if things are going to be too bad and indeed they won't be if you are in the correct position for what is to come.

The view of the economy is going to begin to change. Corporate earnings will begin to falter and all sectors will begin to feel the crunch of deflation which the Federal Reserve Board will have been found to be incapable of reversing. The great debt cloud covering individuals, companies and nations will be shuffled one time too many and someone, somewhere, when we least expect, is going to default and no package in the world is going to be able to stop it. Not even the combined forces of the IMF, World Bank, Federal Reserve and Washington are going to be able to refinance forever.

The Dow Jones Average will be somewhere in the stratosphere when this occurs and investors will begin questioning the amount of economic oxygen at such altitudes. After a quick check they will realize that the oxygen available will only sustain them long enough to get out of their position no matter what the loss.

There will be an erosion of confidence, slowly at first but then spreading to all sectors moving swiftly with drastic consequences. Like a dark storm cloud building over the plains, the thunderhead begins to form slowly at first but then the lightning strikes and the storm is upon us.

Whether founded on a particular failure of the day or simply a growing awareness of the gravity of the economic darkness that surrounds the illusion of a growing economy that has nothing to offer but exploding debt, growing protectionism and falling prices, the erosion of confidence will take hold. Once this erosion has begun there will be no stopping it.

It may begin when some of Wall Street's leaders are found to be out of the market or into short positions. It may come with a major banking failure or a major corporate collapse, although the former is by far the most probable. This collapse will bring with it other major institutions, which in turn bring others down with them and the entire house of cards will finally come tumbling down around us.

As the collapse in the financial markets begins, there will be many who hold on for some time in the belief that what is happening is really just a minor correction. There may even be times where some buying strength comes in and the stock market rebounds for a day or so only to reach new lows the following day. There will be a flight from stocks into bonds and gold which will do extremely well during this period.

A major consideration at this time will be the security of demand deposits in the banking system. Anyone who believes the FDIC or the FSLIC could cover the deposits during a major banking collapse with the number of banks that would entail is doing some wishful thinking. Both the FDIC and the FSLIC are scraping the bottom of the barrel now.

The United States government could conceivably mortgage off the next millennium and put together a package for a rescue but the chances of this are perhaps slim at best. The safe money is not going to be deposited in a bank somewhere. At best you will see only partial reimbursement and this would be after possibly years of litigation to reach a settlement. A banking collapse of any magnitude could greatly affect your assets.

Consider that large brokerage houses are deposited with the major banks that will close their doors during an economic panic. Investors should begin looking closely at how they plan on getting out of the markets and into safe positions. As world prices come down we will enter a more intense period of deflation in the early 90s. Oversupply brought about by overexpansion in virtually every industry is the culprit, not the monetary policy of the Federal Reserve or the central banks of foreign nations.

We have seen prices decline during every long-wave decline

and the period we are entering will be no different no matter what the manipulation of the money supply. We will see a slight increase in inflation late in the 80s due to the surge in activity and the demand brought on by foolish expansion. This will be short-lived as we then drop off the edge of the plateau and into the decline. I should reiterate that we will see dramatic price drops across the board in the early 90s.

Companies will begin closing their doors as business comes to a halt. New companies which are heavily indebted will have no chance of survival. Unemployment will reach highs not seen since the 30s as demand for goods will slow drastically. Many companies will be forced out of business because of the mistakes of others as clients will be incapable of paying their debts for goods purchased.

This is certainly a bleak picture I am painting. We must look beyond the decline as business will go on even during the difficult days ahead and we will all survive in one way or another. We will no doubt learn a great deal about the positive qualities of ourselves and others. These qualities can only be learned from the cooperation necessary during hard and difficult times.

With an occurrence such as the one described above the entire world economy will slow drastically and there will be major changes ushered in. A major collapse of the banking system would be like pulling the plug on a computer system. The entire system would be shut down and when it is plugged back in everything would have been wiped out. Even with major changes, bailouts and restructuring, millions of people will lose everything they own in the coming years.

Contrary to the hopes of many in the Eastern Bloc, this will not mark the end of capitalism but will mark the beginning of a new era which will reach heights previously unimagined. After the excess debt, the inefficiencies and the mismanagement of capital are cleaned from the system as we have seen in every long-wave downturn of the world economy, the true winners and fittest survivors will be prepared to introduce new technology, new ideas and a new respect for hard work.

The capitalist economy will once again be expanding and growing in ways never dreamed possible before the decline. There have been major changes ushered in during every long-wave decline and the coming crash will be no different.

18

A Modern-Day Jubilee

The Kondratieff Wave and the economic evidence in its favor stand alone without the introduction of the concepts and natural laws presented by The Year of Jubilee. Many who study and are convinced of the long-wave cycle base their convictions purely on the evidence of history and documented economic fact. This has been the general approach of this book.

Up to this point we have only lightly touched on the cycle's relationship with Jubilee. In this chapter we will shift gears and take a closer look at the long wave's relation to The Year of Jubilee and the vital role played by human nature. Only by taking a close look at human nature and the precepts presented by The Year of Jubilee can we really gain a clear understanding of the long-wave cycle.

Jubilee gives us the clearest possible insight into why it is that we are of necessity facing a financial collapse and many major economic changes just over the horizon. We should begin by noting that the clear perspective on the long-wave cycle given by Jubilee is centered not in the economic laws it outlines but in its acknowledgement of the flaws in human nature.

At this point we have completed our probe into what Kondratieff had to say about the long wave of economics and we have looked at the great impact of the long wave on history. We have evaluated our current position in relation to the long wave and discussed how we can best profit from our knowledge in the coming years. This brings us to the point where Kondratieff himself was slow to speculate and refused to draw a conclusion.

In an effort to content ourselves with the subject of the Kondratieff long wave we must ask ourselves, "Why?" Are there inherent flaws within our free-market system that force these declines every 50 years or is there an inherent conflict within the people who created and manipulate the system?

Many wonder if the free-market system could ever be a

179

system of perpetual growth and expansion without being flawed with the business cycle both short and long?

These are some of the questions we will examine in this chapter as we look into the nature of the long wave cycle and the free-market system. We will consider how it is that laws written thousands of years ago hold the keys to our understanding the secrets of the long-wave cycle.

Over the past 200 years the free market in its various forms has proven to be the most productive and effective form of economy. The free-market system of today has seen great improvements in wage and labor regulations and has created a more equal society. Our system allows for anyone to work his way up in the system if he is only willing to put forth the effort and the energy necessary.

Many would call what I interpret as the free market to be a very moderate form of socialism. There are some socialist tenets to the reformed free-market system of the late 20th century. However, our economy is still a free-market system at heart and this fact cannot be disputed. I do not want to be accused of reducing the world down to a dualistic economic system of communism and the free market but for all practical purposes the economies of the world are one or the other or something in between.

Why has the free market succeeded so effectively and communism been such an utter failure in terms of output and efficiency? The answer quite simply is in the two system's views of human nature.

The entire free-market system acknowledges that man is basically a proud and self-centered creature. In a free-market system we are aware that in the long run these flaws in human nature create a more cooperating and giving spirit. If these natural tendencies are funneled in a productive direction they make man more able to give and help his fellow man by first finding fulfillment and contentment with himself.

What drives the system is that man wants to do things a little bit better and a little bit more effectively than the guy next door. Man knows that if he succeeds he gains a superior material position and is rewarded substantially in the way of a better life. This makes him more productive in all his endeavors. A system that does not offer a reward in the way of position or advantage to the over-producer and the over-achiever is bound to failure.

If man is not able to accumulate more than he needs, he is

not able to be generous with what he has. A system that does not allow for the accumulation of the material will never be a giving society.

America is the most giving nation in the world because she is the freest nation in the world in terms of economic, religious and political systems.

Communism does not reward the overachiever for his effort but seeks equal treatment for all in relation to the economic system. This is to say that communism gives human nature far too much credit by believing it can create a utopian society of perfect human equality. In a communist system there is no reason to out-perform the next guy because it will not bring any real benefit.

Communism is under the illusion that man actually wants equality in his system. By attempting to force the society into an egalitarian framework, a communist system encourages low productivity.

The free market on the other hand, by acknowledging we do not all have equal ability, allows the over-achiever to express himself which leads to the accumulation of the material. This creates a more productive society and a higher standard of living for everyone. These are of course oversimplifications of the many issues involved and are only meant to give us general guidelines in our comparing and contrasting of communism and the free-market.

There is a drawback to the free-market system which becomes evident in the long-wave cycle. Because man is allowed his freedom in the system, the system has a tendency to get ahead of itself. Man has the tendency to get a little too brave or perhaps a little too greedy so he does things he should not do and takes on more risk than is healthy for the system. This whole process is due directly to man's self-centered nature. The freedom in our economic system allows the participants in the system to go too far in their drive to succeed and get ahead of the next guy. The competitive human spirit generates an explosive fuel that helps to drive the system beyond its healthy boundaries. This is an extremely important element of the sum total of events that creates the great swings in expansion and contraction that cause the long-wave cycle to emerge.

Without the great freedoms we have in the free West, the cycle would be far less drastic but in the same breath the whole system would be far less productive and man would not have made the many advances he has made today. Herein lies the secret to Jeremy Bentham's concept of man finding happiness between two extremes of pain and pleasure. The communist system does not go through great cycles but neither does it advance as quickly as the free market due to the inefficiencies and contradictions built into the communist system.

Many will use the coming decline to speak out against the free-market system and to say it doesn't work properly. These people should take a close look at the alternative and see if they would like to change.

The Kondratieff long-wave cycle forces much-needed change to the system. We will see this with a new monetary system and closer cooperation among nations in the coming years. The long wave acts as a stabilizing element in the political arena and helps to promote social control by its great swing from pleasure to pain. By not allowing society to move in one direction too long, the cycle prevents a state of anarchy.

The long wave is also seen to encourage great religious revival that will strengthen the moral fiber of society. Perhaps above all it purges inefficiency and recklessness out of the economic and social system. Inefficient debt will be forced and purged from the system in the coming years due to vast corporate failures of those who used too much debt to finance operations.

The long wave forces the implementation of new technology and promotes more efficient corporate and manufacturing processes as companies look for new ways to ensure their survival. The long wave keeps the investing world on its toes by making investors realize it is a little more difficult to make a dollar than just by buying stocks as we enter the plateau of the cycle.

All in all the long wave is a balancing element for every area and aspect of free-market society and should not be used to question the validity of or to condemn the system. In a strange but very real way the long-wave cycle should be deeply appreciated.

I gave a brief presentation of The Year of Jubilee in the introduction. Here we will take a closer look at Jubilee in an attempt to better understand our system's faults.

The relationship between the Kondratieff long-wave cycle and The Year of Jubilee is truly fascinating.

The Year of Jubilee was a time of celebration as well as being an economic law that was to be enforced every 50 years in the nation of Israel according to the writings of Moses in Leviticus 25:8-55. This economic law had the effect of discounting prices against year 50 which was to be the Year of Jubilee. The value of land was figured by how much it could be used until The Year of Jubilee.

The closer you were to The Year of Jubilee the cheaper you could purchase land which was the chief means of production in those days. This would have the effect of giving us the exact opposite of what we see in the Kondratieff long wave. In the long wave we have prices beginning low after a crash and a decline and moving constantly higher until they fall with the long-wave decline.

A system which incorporated The Year of Jubilee would have the highest prices for the means of production in year one following The Year of Jubilee and the prices would constantly fall until year 50 or the next Year of Jubilee. This would bring great stability to the production process. The flow of capital in a Jubilee system would be smooth and efficient. A Jubilee system would bring stability to all aspects of society by forcing the redistribution of generated wealth every 50 years.

The first two cycles of the long wave were basically up 25 years and then down 25 years. As we have moved to a more centralized and world economy we have moved more towards a lengthy advance and a sharp decline in the long wave.

This was seen clearly with the Great Depression. The Great Depression came later than the other declines and was far sharper and more severe than other declines in long-wave history. The current advance is the longest in the history of the long-wave cycle.

It should be remembered that the decade of the 1980s is the plateau period and the late 80s will see the long-wave peak in the financial markets while the early 80s saw the peak in capital expansion.

This is of great interest in light of our discussion in chapter four on the role played by the emergence of today's world economy on the long-wave cycle.

The Year of Jubilee was a law for one single economy, not a divided world economy. The growing strength of the world economy has created the phenomenon of a longer long-wave advance by increasing the interrelationship and interdependence of the nations of the world.

This gives the economy more stability and allows prices and debt to keep climbing to levels they could not have reached in the first two cycles. The more interrelated the world economy the longer the advance of the long wave can be with a maximum advance of some 50 years.

The point of instability came much earlier in the first two cycles so the decline came far sooner. As we have seen the centralized world economy growing in strength we see the long wave reaching the inverse of The Year of Jubilee system. This is to say that as the world economy grows more interrelated we are beginning to see a 50-year advance in the long wave and a sharp decline.

The decline will last five to 10 years depending on the actions taken to relieve the collapse. Jubilee was a one-year transition while our system, because of inverting the law, takes quite a few years to get out of its decline. From such a hypothesis we could say that by the late 1990s we should be well into another long-wave advance and, if the western free-market system is still in operation we should see another major downturn around the year 2050.

Another interesting part of the laws for The Year of Jubilee was that all debts would be eliminated in the 50th year. This prevented a build-up of inefficient and dangerous debt levels in the economy. Loans would not be made with maturities beyond The Year of Jubilee because they would not be repaid. Debt was unable to snowball and be refinanced as we see in our system today. There would be a tendency for more debt early in the cycle in a Jubilee system whereas you have more debt late in the free-market system of today.

Outstanding debt was constantly decreasing in a Jubilee system as production prices decreased. Debt can be a very useful tool in our economy but it is clear that too much of a good thing can be disastrous. Debt is at unprecedented levels in every sector of the economy at the present time, just as we saw in the 20s. At this same point in a Jubilee system, debt would be virtually nonexistent. Debt is not inherently evil in and of itself but when used as indiscriminately as it is in our system it is bound to eventually create problems. Slavery was a form of indebtedness so all slaves were freed in The Year of Jubilee.

We are all aware that the laws for The Year of Jubilee would not work in our modern system by any stretch of the imagination. This is not why we are observing the Jubilee system. The Year of Jubilee acknowledged and constrained the elements of human nature that would cause the system to get out of control. Jubilee acted as a safety valve for the system to prevent it from building up too much pressure. In the modern free-market system we simply have the long-wave decline to relieve the pressure. The principles of The Year of Jubilee give us a number of clues as to our own system's faults and why it lets off steam every 50 years or so.

By looking at The Year of Jubilee, we more clearly understand why it is that our system overexpands and overproduces. By controlling prices and thus inflation and by forcing the elimination of debt by year 50, the Jubilee system would be stabilized and would not be forced to decline every 50 years as is our system.

An understanding of Jubilee helps us to gain insight into why the free-market process creates too much debt and ignites inflation and why these factors combine to help produce the long-wave cycle. Unlike The Year of Jubilee, very few find reason for celebration when our system enters its decline.

There are those who believe the free-market system will one day no longer have a cycle, short or long, but will be in a perpetual state of slow but stable growth. Those who believe this have the notion of perfectibility for the free market which stems from the belief of the perfectibility of human nature.

This is where their ideas are flawed. Human nature is not perfectible in terms of its pride and greed and so the system that gains its vitality and strength from this nature will never reach a state of perfection without flaws or cycles. A system that tried to produce perfect and stable growth would be caught in the same trap of communism and would have to have so many controls and regulations to maintain stability it would produce only stagnation.

Man must be free to fail as well as to succeed in order to produce the growth and success we have in the free-market system. As man is free to move from a state of risk-aversion to a state of risk-proneness, he creates the business cycle. If the system ever did reach a state of equilibrium and constant growth, man would most likely find himself very bored.

There is a twist to the nature of man that loves to take risk. This risk element in human nature contributes a great deal to the long-wave cycle. There have been a number of studies in recent years into why the United States is such a productive nation. Many believe that there is a biological or hereditary factor in people that make them willing to take risk.

Consider the sort of person who would pull up stakes and move to a newly discovered nation as did our ancestors as they came to America. This sort of risk appreciation and enjoyment is still in our blood today and makes us the economic power we are. Our appreciation of risk gives a powerful forward thrust to our economic system. However, it is this desire and willingness to take risks that forces the free-market system to overexpand itself and thus eventually produces the long-wave cycle.

This is not limited to the United States. It is part of the free-market western world and is part of the reason that the long-wave exists. A controlled society that sought to eliminate the cycle would have to suppress the desire to assume risk and would thus stifle productivity. Yes, the business cycle could be eliminated with many restrictions and regulations, but this would not be the sort of system you or I would enjoy and appreciate.

The concept of equilibrium is that we are allowed and able to move too far in one direction or too far in the other and thus we tend towards the center for our own safety.

A quick comparison of micro and macro economics gives us a feel for the argument of allowing the free-market system to be granted the freedom to take its natural course.

The idea of price being an equilibrium between supply and demand gives an excellent illustration of the forces that create the long wave. Just as price fixing creates confusion and inefficiency in the economy by attempting to force stability, so any effort to eliminate the business cycle by forced rules and regulations would breed confusion and stagnation in the entire economy. As prices are allowed to float freely from one direction to another or one extreme to another in order to find equilibrium, so the free-market system must be allowed to flow from one extreme to the other in the long wave to reach its own unique and broadly based equilibrium.

Only by allowing freedom of movement from one extreme to the other can we find equilibrium. The free market must be allowed to take its course unconstrained and unregulated if it is to be productive and competitive and provide the highest possible standard of living for the world. The system isn't perfect — but then neither is man, which is why the system works.

Of course we would hope that in the future, when a more clear and decisive history of the long wave is available, that we would learn from our mistakes and begin making adjustments to make the cycle less devastating.

In this book we have looked at past civilizations and looked at the factors which led to their demise. We have looked closely at the history of the free-market system we have today, both its qualities and drawbacks. We have taken a close look at the work of the Russian economist Nikolai D. Kondratieff and what he saw in the data he had gathered on the long wave in free-market economies.

We have come to realize that Kondratieff could not as fully appreciate the long-wave cycle as we are able to due to our experiences of this century. The emergence of a world economy has given us a unique look into the long-wave cycle and its character.

Psychology has shown a powerful relationship between the long wave and how society relates to the economic world and what people expect and anticipate from the system.

We have seen that man's conflict with his fellow man is directly related to his economic circumstances and surroundings as war is far more likely during a time of expanding economies than contracting declining ones.

We have taken a look at the banking system and the condition the system was in during past peaks of the long-wave cycle and how similar those conditions are compared to our banking system today.

We have looked closely at the forces at work in the long wave and their enormous impact on world trade.

We have realized that the worsening situation of agriculture today is not an isolated incident to history but parallels all declines of the long-wave cycle in the past.

Technology and invention have been seen as important elements to both the long-wave expansion and the long-wave contraction as man seeks to find solutions to his economic condition. The political atmosphere of the day has been seen to have a direct relationship and be enormously influenced by the location in which we find ourselves in the long wave.

Our study of the long wave has brought us to the basic investment instruments of gold, stocks, bonds and real estate as we have speculated on how we could best profit from the long-wave cycle and its effect on the economy.

We attempted to draw a scenario of what to expect and what to look for in the coming years of the late 80s as we find ourselves once again on the plateau of the long-wave cycle.

We have speculated as to the great changes that will be ushered in during the coming years as the free-market system is once again pushed over the edge of instability and brought into a time of confusion and questioning as to its faults. Lastly we have taken a look at the nature of the free-market system and its relation to human nature and The Year of Jubilee.

In the process, we reviewed the inherent problems or perhaps qualities that lead our system into a period of contraction and collapse.

All in all we have taken a good look at the evidence available and are now brought to a point of decision as to our acceptance or rejection of the long-wave hypothesis. The evidence is overpowering in favor of acceptance but the true test will lie in the next 10 years of economic reality.

In closing I would like to again emphasize the most positive aspect of the long-wave cycle. This is the great opportunity that presents itself to the astute investor to use the coming decline for his advantage and gain by his awareness of the reaction of the various investment instruments in the marketplace.

The next few years will prove to make a great many investors extremely wealthy while at the same time they will remove a far larger number from those same ranks.

All who are aware of the Kondratieff Wave or long-wave cycle should be in the former group if they are not consumed by greed and brought down with the rest of the economy by holding on "just a little bit longer."

With a good knowledge of the long-wave cycle, the coming years offer the investor the perfect opportunity to have a modern day celebration of The Year of Jubilee.

Above all we must always remember that human nature is imperfect and we will never create a perfect economic or social system. The clear evidence of human imperfection makes us aware and accountable to the fact that every human soul stands in need of redemption by its creator.

THE KNOXX FINANCIAL REPORT is a
monthly investment advisory newsletter
based on long-wave and fundamental research. The KFR will keep you in touch
and up-to-date with the financial, economic, and political issues presented in this
book. For a one-month trial issue, send $3.

The Knoxx Corporation
Box 400
Medford, North Carolina 28757

Bibliography

Chapters One and Two

Lightner, Otto C. *The History of Business Depressions*. New York: Burt Franklin, 1922.

Chapter Three

Kondratieff, Nikolai D. "The Long Waves In Economic Life." In *Readings in Business Cycle Theory*. New York: AMS Press, 1951.

Chapter Four

Macklin, Gordon S. "The NASDAQ Perspective on the World Equity Market" In *Vital Speeches*. January, 1986.

Chapter Five

Stoken, Dick. "The Kondratieff Cycle and its Effects on Social Psychology." In *The Futurist*. February, 1980.

Chapter Six

Encyclopedia Americana. New York. (Used for research on Wars)

Levy, Jack S. *War in the Modern Great Power System, 1495-1975*. Lexington: University Press of Kentucky, 1983.

Martino, Joseph P. "Does the Kondratieff Wave Really Exist?" In *The Futurist*. February 1985.

Chapter Seven

Clausen, A.W. "Third World Debt and Global Recovery." In *Vital Speeches*. April 1983.

Feinberg, Andrew. "The Crash of 1989." In *Gentlemens Quarterly*. February 1987.

Hindle, Tim. "Banking's House of Cards." In *World Press Review*. May 1982.

Holzach, Robert. "The International Credit Crisis." In *Vital Speeches*. August 1983.

Kennedy, Susan Estabrook. *The Banking Crisis of 1933*. Lexington: University Press of Kentucky, 1973.

Malabre, Alfred L. "Debt Keeps Growing, With Major Risk in the Private Sector." In *The Wall Street Journal*. February 2, 1987.

Simmons. "Washington Memo: Worst-Case Scenario." In *Financial World*. October 15, 1983.

Snyder, Julian M. "An Economic Theory for the Real World." In *Vital Speeches*. Southold N.Y.: City News Publishing Co., August 1983.

Woche, Wutschafts. "Banking Crisis Ahead?" In *World Press Review*. N.Y.: The Stanley Foundation. November 1982.

Yamani, Ahmed Zaki. "Control and Decontrol in the Oil Market." In *Vital Speeches*. June 1983.

Chapter Eight

Andres, William A. "The Case for Open Trade" In *Vital Speeches*. August, 1985.

Eckes, Alfred E. "International Trade in Turbulent Times" In *Vital Speeches*. July, 1985.

Henske, John M. "The Changing World Enviroment for International Trade." In *Vital Speeches*. October 1982.

Porter, Roger B. "International Economic Challenges of the 1980's" In *Vital Speeches*. January, 1983.

Peterson, David. "Neo-Conservatism." In *Vital Speeches*. February 1987.

Whalley, John. *Trade Liberalization among Major World Trading Areas*. Cambridge: The MIT Press, 1985.

Wilson, John Oliver. "Trade Wars." In *Vital Speeches*. June 1985.

Chapter Nine

Lodwick, Seeley G. "Are Farmers on the Way Out?" In *Vital Speeches*. June 1983.

McCormick, John. "A Riches-to-Rags Story" In *Newsweek*. April 2, 1984.

Sheets, Kenneth R. "Farmers up in Arms" In *U.S. News and World Report*. March 11, 1985.

Sheets, Kenneth R. "Ailing Farm Economy — Damage Spreads Wide" In *U.S. News and World Report*. July 29, 1985.

Wall, Wendy L. "U.S. Agriculture Faces Still More Shrinkage, Many Economists Say" In *The Wall Street Journal*. December 24, 1986.

Chapter Ten

Dula, Arthur M. "American Business: Heading into Orbit." In *Saturday Evening Post*. March 1985.

Mandel, Ernest. *Long Waves of Capitalist Development*. Cambridge: Cambridge University Press. 1980.

Reynolds, Alan. "In Search of a Money Standard" In *The Wall Street Journal*. November 12, 1985.

Schmookler, Jacob. *Invention and Economic Growth*. Cambridge: Harvard University Press. 1966.

Wriston, Walter. "In Search of a Money Standard" In *The Wall Street Journal*. November 12, 1985.

Chapter Thirteen

Feinberg, Andrew. "The Crash of 1989." In *Gentlemens Quarterly*. February 1987.

Leffler, George L. *The Stock Market:* The Ronald Press Company. New York. 1957.

Malabre, Alfred L. "Kondratieff Rolls On, As Does the Economy" In *The Wall Street Journal*. January 20, 1986.

Sherrid, Pamela. "The Great Bull Market of 1985" In *U.S. News and World Report*. December 16, 1985.

Chapter Fourteen

Homer, Sidney. *A History of Interest Rates:* Rutgers University Press. New Brunswick. 1963.

Chapter Fifteen

Green, Timothy. *The New World of Gold*. New York: Walker and Company. 1981.

Paul, Ron. *Case for Gold*. Washington: Cato Institute. 1982.

Chapter Sixteen

Waldman, Peter. "Severe Deflation Hits Commercial Properties In Many Areas of U.S." In *The Wall Street Journal*. September 4, 1986.